Praise for *On a Street Called Easy,*
I...

"Hilarious. . . . Prose as well crafted as the mansion's heart-pine beams makes this ode to Joye and its colorful history an engrossing blueprint for anyone with a dollar—give or take half a million—and a dream. 'A' "—*Entertainment Weekly*

"A gutsy pair of writers + a run-down 60-room hulk = a true-life tale of comically inept contractors and nosy neighbors."—*People*

"An enchanting chronicle. . . . The often hilarious narrative details the major and minor pitfalls of two novice rehabbers and their comic cast of contractors and laborers. . . . Absolutely charming."—*Booklist*

"A 'restoration comedy' almost as rich as the history of the house. . . . Sure to delight, even if your home-improvement skills make Lucy Ricardo look like Bob Vila."—*The Columbia, South Carolina State*

"Sharp, entertaining tales filled with robust portraits of place, wonderfully particularized figures, and great enthusiasm." —*Historic Preservation*

"A deft, amusing look at history, life and people in a small southern town, as well as at a large-scale adventure in renovation."—*Kirkus Reviews*

ALSO BY GREGORY WHITE SMITH AND STEVEN NAIFEH

The Mormon Murders
Jackson Pollock: An American Saga
Final Justice
A Stranger in the Family

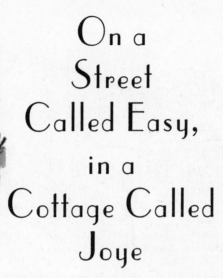

On a Street Called Easy, in a Cottage Called Joye

by

GREGORY WHITE SMITH

and STEVEN NAIFEH

Illustrations by DANIEL BAXTER

Broadway Books **New York**

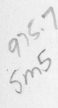

To
JOSEPH HARTZLER
and
KIKI MURPHY BLALOCK

Memories make a house a home;
Old friends make a lifetime a life.

Contents

Part Two   A Big Job

Part Three   Getting Acquainted

Part Four All Balled Up

Epilogue At Home

Notice

This is a true story. Some names and identifying details have been changed to protect the innocent, the ignorant, the incompetent, the venal, and the litigious — and the authors from all of the above. In a few places, the sequence of events has been altered and time compressed, but if you wanted history unmilled, you would buy one of those big, dusty books in the back of the store; and if you preferred life unedited, you wouldn't bother with books at all.

As a convenience to the reader, we have written the book from Greg's point of view to avoid the awkwardness and confusion typical of jointly authored autobiographical books. But don't be fooled. This book, like all our others, is, from beginning to end, a joint endeavor.

GREG SMITH
STEVE NAIFEH

Part One **Fantasy Island**

1.

Palaces in the Air

I always wanted to live in a palace.

As far back as I can remember, to the sepia days when fantasy, ambition, and tomorrow were indistinguishable, I saw myself residing in splendor someday. My first toy, or at least the first I remember, was a green mesh bag filled with wooden blocks — red rectangles, yellow columns, and blue posts — with which I built sprawling palaces in primary splendor.

When my fingers grew less blunt, I graduated to the little interlocking red plastic bricks. They came in cardboard tubes, I recall, but only enough in one tube for a modest saltbox with two doors and a lousy dozen windows. I wheedled tube after tube out of my parents until I had filled an old television box with the little plastic chips, enough to keep me busy for days covering the living room floor with the vast brick saltbox of my dreams.

Seeing my interest and boundless energy, and hoping, I suppose, to turn me into another Robert Moses, my parents bought me "skyscraper blocks," little vertical sections of Empire State Building facade in white plastic that could be stuck together to create buildings taller than their creator. But I wasn't fooled. I took the blocks and built *out*, not up, creating vast Persian pleasure domes of gleaming white plastic that reached into the dining room and beyond, to the very threshold of the kitchen door.

On summer trips to my grandparents' farm near Grenada, Mississippi, I would trek with my cousin Bub to a nearby creek bed and build huge sand castles on the shallow slopes of a cattle cut. Not castles, really. Tutored by Bub, a bookish older boy of vast learning and exquisite sensibilities, I fashioned seaside "villas" (a delicious new word) fit for a Roman emperor. By dribbling wet sand scooped from the creek bottom, I created stepped parterres surrounded by balustrades and intricate colonnaded facades crowned with statuary. Then, without warning, my grandfather would drive his cattle through the cut, and all that architectural splendor would be trampled under hoof.

My own circumstances at the time fell somewhere short of imperial. From a small, nondescript house on a nondescript street (appropriately named Fair Avenue) in the nondescript city of Columbus, Ohio, I knew little of the lifestyles of the rich and famous. The closest I came was on my daily bike rides to and from school when I passed through the toniest neighborhood in town, Bexley. Every morning and every afternoon, I took a different zigzag route through the blocks of mostly mock Tudor and Colonial mansions, on tree-lined streets with names like Drexel and Parkview, hoping for the open door or parted curtain that would give me a rare peek at life inside those enchanted castles. I especially liked riding around at night, when every uncurtained window became an amber-lit display case. I was lucky, I suppose, not to be mistaken for a Peeping Tom by the gentry I glimpsed on these nocturnal tours. They had no way of knowing I was more interested in the linen-fold paneling on the wall than in what went on between the linens on the bed.

So eager was I to see inside the showplaces of the midwestern mercantile class that whenever one of the big houses on my route came up for sale, I would wait until it was empty (usually after it was sold, on a weekend during renovations) and break in. Although actual "breaking" was rarely required, given negligent workmen, the chaos of construction, and the generally lax security standards of the era, I remember fondly the furtive thrill of wandering forbidden through a grand, strange, empty house. Over the years, I saw many of the best homes in Bexley that way. To this day, the smell of sawdust and paint brings on a little illicit rush of adrenaline.

By the time I was ten, I had started drawing my fantasies. On big sheets of paper, in meticulous detail, I rendered the houses of my longing. First in floor plans, floor by floor, hundreds of rooms to the floor, each one carefully labeled

("BR" for ballroom or billiard room or bathroom; "SR" for servant's room, of which there were scores; and tiny little "CL"s everywhere); then in elevations, great assemblages of architectural details — porticoes, bay windows, dormers, gables, turrets, and balconies — details borrowed from the big houses I passed every morning, piled high like wedding cakes, Tudor flavor or Colonial revival, every stone or brick or clapboard carefully drawn and shaded with the side of a pencil.

Well into my teens, I kept these drawings under my bed, showing them to no one, pulling them out now and then in the privacy of bedtime to seed my dreams.

At some point, I suppose, I must have gritted my teeth and conceded that such a foolish childhood dream would never come true, that I would never get to live in a palace after all. Like my friend in third grade who dreamed of being a king someday only to discover that kings were born not made, I must have concluded somewhere along the way that there wasn't much point in wishing for such a thing. Eventually, the elaborate drawings were packed away with other childhood memorabilia, and I went off to college and law school and reality.

But the dream wouldn't go away.

I still craned my neck to peer longingly down every gated driveway I passed; still devoured every issue of *House & Garden* and *Architectural Digest;* still haunted the real estate showroom at Sotheby's; still tore through the *Times* every week to revel for a few glorious, glossy minutes in the "Luxury Homes and Estates" section of the Sunday magazine. Even after I turned away from a career in law, which might have afforded me at least a sturdy brick manse with slate roof and leaded-glass windows in a Greenwich-like suburb, and decided to make my living as a writer — a garret-bound, fifth-floor-walk-up, cold-water-flat, rent-controlled writer — I *still* couldn't shake the dream.

And then, suddenly, it came true.

2.

Two of a Kind

How did a struggling New York writer with no family money, no connections, and no criminal propensities get to live out the fantasy of every furtive riffler of *House & Garden?*

The first step was to find somebody *else* as house-crazy as I was.

When we met on the first day of law school, I had no way of knowing that Steve would meet that essential requirement. We couldn't have come from more different backgrounds. While I was bicycling through the *Leave It to Beaver* streets of Columbus, Ohio, Steve was following his diplomat parents from one unlikely exotic locale to another: Tehran, Iran; Amman, Jordan; Karachi, Pakistan; Lagos, Nigeria; Tulsa, Oklahoma. By the time he entered law school, he had lived in *forty-eight* different houses. I had lived in three.

While bouncing around, however, Steve had had a chance to see things I never saw in Bexley: the Louvre and Versailles, the Hermitage and Petrovorets, Buckingham Palace and the British Museum, the Escorial and the Prado. While I was peering in the windows of the country club bourgeoisie, Steve was walking through the Hall of Mirrors in the steps of the Sun King. While I was fantasizing about converting the Capitol building in Washington (the biggest building I'd ever seen) to single-family use, Steve was imagining what it would be like to banish all those intrusive tourists from the Hermitage and take up where the last czar left off.

Once, when Steve was in grade school in Benghazi, Libya, a teacher asked the class to write a report on the topic "If you had only one wish, what would you wish for?" To her great dismay, only one student asked for world peace. Most wished for hot rods, or party dresses, or trips home. And then there was the one little boy who wished for a huge piece of the Alaskan wilderness surrounding a single house as grand as Versailles — only five times bigger.

3.

A Hell of a Town

So how did *two* struggling writers with no family money, no connections, and no criminal propensities get to live out the fantasy of every *Architectural Digest* addict?

It started with a trip to the Xerox center — a sure way to make one rethink the meaning of life — on a gray and rainy Saturday in New York in the summer of 1988. Defying the weather and all reason, Steve and I left our apartment in a triumphant mood that morning. At about four o'clock earlier the same morning, we had put the bleary-eyed finishing touches on the sixteen-hundred-page manuscript of *Jackson Pollock,* a biography of the abstract expressionist painter —

an effort that had vacuumed up the better part of our thirties.

At the copy center on Broadway, we waited in line for
what seemed like an hour (which, in New York, can be as little as ten minutes) while the impresario of a neighborhood
vegetarian modern-dance company explained to the lone,
bored Bengali attendant the "visual concept" behind a flyer
announcing the troupe's next free concert; then, with great
solemnity and at great length, pondered the metaphysical
implications of paper color: white, pink, baby blue, or buff?

Next, we stopped at the bank, where I stood lookout on
the street while Steve withdrew some cash from an ATM
machine. The bank's lobby had been converted into a video
arcade of automated tellers that was crowded on Saturday
morning and usually bust by Sunday night. A contingent of
questionable types hung around the entrance at all times,
causing customers to fumble nervously for their cards to
gain admittance and then hurry through when the door
buzzed open.

At the pharmacy, I was informed that my prescription
had expired.

"Could I have the doctor call it in?" I asked.

"No," the pharmacist said. "Prescriptions for drugs like
this have to be in writing. In triplicate. State law."

"Could I have a couple of pills to tide me over the weekend until I can see the doctor again?"

"No," he said with a shrug. "My hands are tied. State
law."

Could he give me a less-perilous substitute?

"Absolutely not!" he exulted.

I pointed out that we had just passed a man on the street

outside who was obviously prepared to sell me any drug I wanted: no prescription, no triplicate, no expiration, no questions. Indeed, it was easier to get heroin on the corner than antihistamine in his store.

"Not my problem," he said with another shrug.

It had started to rain, and by the time Steve and I reached the safety of the canopy of our apartment building on Central Park West, we were drenched. In the lobby, we found the yellow-haired man from G elevator nestled in his usual seat on the sofa smoking his usual loathsome cigar. Mr. G's wife had forbidden smoking in their apartment, so Mr. G had *no choice* but to come downstairs and share his loathsome habit with the rest of us.

Steve and I shared a four-room apartment in the El Dorado, a magnificent sandstone art deco confection overlooking Central Park, only our apartment was at the back of the building (of course), overlooking not the park but a sunless concrete cavity formed by the butting rears of the brownstone townhouses on 90th and 91st Streets. The real estate agent who sold us the place called this crevice "a Parisian postage-stamp park" (which, of course, meant she could advertise it as having a "park view"), although, surrounded by high metal fencing and curls of concertina wire, it looked less like a park than an outpost on the Maginot Line.

As we entered the apartment, soaked, our "park" echoed with the ominous sound of children's laughter, nature's car alarm, the kind of mischievous, conspiratorial laughter that is almost always at someone's expense. On this day, ours. It seemed the children of the park had learned a new game: throwing pebbles at the windows of the big apartment building next door, and ours were among the few windows low enough for adolescent arm muscles but high enough for sport. Shards of glass littered our living room floor.

When I shouted the ritual threats from the jagged window, the children giggled and shrugged their shoulders. They knew I wasn't about to cross the line of iron fencing and concertina wire. The super told us it would be several weeks before he could replace the windows. A local glazier demanded fifty bucks a window (per pane, that is) and when I balked said he didn't have time anyway and slammed the phone down.

It wasn't even Saturday noon, and we were already Sunday-night fed up with New York.

In that spirit, we sought refuge across town in that bastion of escapist fantasies, Sotheby's. It was there, that day, between Javanese bodhisattvas and English silver epergnes, during a rejuvenating rustle through the racks of Sotheby's real estate section, that we first saw Joye Cottage.

4.

Mr. Whitney's Winter Cottage

It was anything but a "cottage." *"Sixty rooms,"* the brochure swooned. *"20,000 square feet of living space!"* Even among the rows of mammoth Texas tract mansions, Greenwich grandiosities, oversexed Malibu beach houses, and Philadelphia faux châteaux, even in this gallery of *grandes maisons*, this one stood out. *"Sixty rooms, 18 bedrooms, 12 baths, 12 staff bedrooms, 4 staff baths."* Built a century ago by robber baron William C. Whitney, this was the kind of "cottage" I had built on the living room floor. The color pictures showed sweeping white colonnades set against a skyline of immense greenery, a reflecting pool rimmed with flowers, Greek porticoes framed by iron gates, a magnificent front hall adorned with wainscoting, pilasters, and columns. This wasn't a cottage any more than the Petit Trianon was really petit or the White House was really a house. This was a cottage in the Newport sense, like The Breakers or The Elms. In short, this was a palace.

Gracious country estate . . . landscaped grounds lush with Southern vegetation, white columns, expansive 100-foot veranda facing formal garden and pool . . . sweeping lawns framed by towering oaks and pines . . . timeless appeal . . . the very legacy of understated classic design . . . the essence of American aristocratic style!

In Sotheby's, in the rain, in a rapture of fantasy, we read and reread the fine print:

MAIN HOUSE: *salon, billiard room, den, and 7 bedrooms, each with fireplace and full bath. The salon is paneled with three-quarter-height wainscoting, and an exposed beam ceiling, freestanding Ionic columns and pilasters . . . elliptical arch framed by pilasters leads to a double-rung, open stringer staircase with paneled newel posts topped with classical urns.*

SOUTHWEST WING: *connected to the main house by a glassed-in colonnade, 3 bedrooms, fireplaces, and baths . . . 3 staff bedrooms upstairs.*

SOUTHEAST WING: *6 family bedrooms each with full bath and wood-burning fireplace . . . 2 sitting rooms . . . 2 staff bedrooms.*

NORTHWEST WING: *double-height ballroom . . . bedroom and bath . . . 2 staff bedrooms upstairs.*

NORTHEAST WING: *dining room windowed on 3 sides highlighted by a vast delft tile fireplace . . . butlers' pantry . . . original cabinets with glass diamond-paned doors . . . kitchen pantry . . . laundry and staff dining room . . . 8 staff bedrooms.*

Finally, breathlessly, we reached the last line: *"Offered at $1,700,000."*

We put the brochure down and, unable to find a cab, walked home in the rain.

For days afterward, Steve and I dragged around the four dark rooms of our bunker by the park, glaring into the treeless, sunless concrete gulch of our Parisian backyard, unable to get the images of Joye Cottage out of our heads: the sun-washed porches, the eternity of leaves, the virgin white clapboard surrounded by jade-green lawns, fluted columns, and iron lace . . .

Finally, we gave in. We had to go there. We had to see it.

Some might call it a lark. Others, just temporary insanity. Buying such a pleasure dome was out of the question, no matter how irresistible its allure. The apartment on Central Park West was the only asset we owned, and we were lucky to have that. Five years before, at a time when the real estate market was down, we had fallen into our first (and biggest) commercial success, a book called *How to Make Love to a Woman*. About the same time, we stumbled into the office of a female banker who thrilled at the prospect of working with the authors of a book she had not only heard about but actually read and, in fact, held in orgasmically high esteem.

We had no reason to believe that *Jackson Pollock* could work similar miracles on the financial institutions of the South.

Nevertheless, a week later, July Fourth weekend, in the middle of a thundering rainstorm, we drove into Aiken, South Carolina.

At 9:00 P.M. the streets were empty.

Steve and I had spent our last ten years in New York City, most of those years — the waking hours, at least — in darkness: in the antic hours between 6:00 P.M. and 6:00 A.M. when we did most of our writing. We were accustomed to going to bed as the sun rose and, in winter, waking up as it set; accustomed to late-night sorties from our pillbox on Central Park West down Columbus Avenue; accustomed to the sidewalk parade of overcooked personae, the beehive bars and Korean delis, the bright lunatic assaults of store windows, and, of course, the danger.

Clearly, we were not in New York anymore.

I took my foot off the accelerator in order not to miss anything. The car slowed to a crawl. There wasn't anything to miss. No people. No lights. A minute later the town disappeared behind us. We turned around and stopped at the first motel we saw. We banged on the door to roust a sleeping night watchman who doubled as the check-in clerk after ten. After he grudgingly gave us a key, we set out again in search of the fantasy that had lured us a thousand miles out of our safe bunker, guided only by the light of an emerging full moon and a kind of witch-hazel sense of direction: a feeling that maybe, just maybe, we were destined to own this house, and if so, then surely we could find it.

A half hour later, we stopped to ask directions at the only establishment still open, a gas-station-cum-junk-food-cum-video-rental emporium with a honky-tonk bar in back. We told the night clerk, a jowly, amiable man with the gray, grizzled look of a recovering alcoholic, that we were looking for Joye Cottage. Did he know where it was?

"Never heard of it," he said, very amiably.

Steve thought more explanation might be helpful. "It's a great big, sixty-room place. . . ."

The man looked thoughtfully off into space. "Nope," he finally said, "doesn't ring a bell."

"The old Whitney-Vanderbilt estate?" Steve persisted.

Another thoughtful, conscientious vacant look. "Nope."

Steve grew agitated (it had been a long trip). "Lots of columns and porticoes around a central courtyard, all white . . ."

The man lifted his steel-gray fishing hat and smoothed back a few strands of silver hair, clearly straining himself. "Well, come to think of it," he finally said, "maybe I have heard of it." He waved his hand in a general sort of way. "Try up the street."

Steve pressed him to be more specific.

"You see that road out there?" he began, focusing mightily. "That's Whiskey Road."

"Whiskey?" Steve and I echoed.

"That's right," he said wistfully. "Whiskey. You go down Whiskey and turn left at the second light."

"What's the name of the street?" I asked.

"Oh, that's easy," he said.

"I'm sure it is," I said, "but we're from out of town."

"No, it really is easy," he insisted.

"Easy for you, maybe." I was getting impatient.

"No," he said, "the *name* is Easy."

"Okay, okay," I fumed, "second left," and stormed out the door.

The second left off Whiskey Road, was, indeed, easy — Easy Street, that is. And that's where we found it.

The house filled the moonlit horizon. From a dark stand of pines at one end, it emerged as from a cave: long, ghostly temple walls, a Doric portico, a glassed-in colonnade, two high, massive gables, a balustrade in the air, a long, hipped roof, a glimpse of dormers, the curve of pagoda eaves; dozens of blacked-out windows: in bays, in half rounds and ovals, in arrays of tiny diamond panes and huge sheets, their old, flawed glass queering the light from our headlamps. The facade stretched from darkness to darkness, the ends so far distant from the center they disappeared altogether. Sitting on a high, brick foundation, the whole seemed to float in shadow, like some grand architectural ghost come back from the other side of demolition to cold-kiss its old foundations and mock the wrecking ball.

The next morning, before meeting the real estate agent, we explored the town of Aiken. For the house, we at least had pictures to go by; the town, on the other hand, could have been anything: an industrial wasteland, a rural ghost town, a boondocks Brigadoon. The Sotheby's brochure had said only that it was eighteen miles from Augusta, Georgia, on the other side of the Savannah River. But where was Augusta, Georgia? (Neither of us was a golfer, you see.) For that matter, where was the Savannah River? To answer those questions, we had to unearth our big *Times* atlas. It was there, all right, a tiny speck of a town just off Interstate 20 between Atlanta and Charlotte. Could we live *there?* We flipped back and forth between the full-page map of New York City and that elusive speck in the belly of South Carolina. Could we move from there to *there?*

That morning, the answer was all around us — in the bright Carolina sunlight, in the broad parkways lined with ancient oaks and grand clapboard houses, in the vast, rolling fields where horses grazed, and in the quaint clay streets where cars yielded to carriages. We turned down one street and found ourselves heading straight into a huge old elm tree, twenty feet around, that stood defiantly in the middle of the road, exactly where it had stood for a century before they laid the road around it. We didn't know until much later that these quiet, verdant streets had been the playground of the rich for a century, or that those rolling fields were prime Thoroughbred training country, but we could see in the vast stables and racetracks of red Georgia clay, in the great clearings of polo fields and golf courses (eight of each), that this was a town where air was more important than air rights, and trees took precedence over traffic flow.

Yes. We could live here.

The house, unfortunately, was another matter. In that same beautiful Carolina sunlight, we discovered that Joye Cottage was neither the southern Eden described in the Sotheby's brochure, nor the fairy castle that had appeared out of the mist the night before. Our guide was Wilma Hazlett, a sharp-eyed, raven-haired woman in her thirties, whose local real estate agency had listed the house with Sotheby's. Showing a sixty-room house wasn't easy, and Wilma, although determinedly courteous, clearly had her doubts that we were worth the effort. Her long experience in *not* selling the house had left her profoundly skeptical about the prospects of success, and she rattled off the house's flaws with a fatalistic candor — a kind of perverse, reverse sales pitch: None of the sixty rooms was adequately heated or air-conditioned. Except for an odd piece here and there, the house was completely unfurnished. None of the sixteen bathrooms had a shower. Only one had a functioning toilet. The ancient coal-black gas stove in the kitchen hadn't worked in a decade. The only refrigerator in the house was a "pie safe" built into the pantry and cooled by a hole in the floor to the basement. The roof leaked. Diluvially. Indeed, we should be careful where we stood when it rained, Wilma warned. Depending on the spot, we could simply get wet or, worse, get crushed by one of the big roundels of rotten plaster that fell from the ceiling every now and then without warning. Any questions?

When we finished the tour, Wilma sighed, as if relieved that we had made it through without serious bodily injury, then asked in a flat, resigned voice, as if she knew what the answer would be, "So what do you think?"

Steve and I looked at each other and said in perfect unison, "We love it!"

We had found our palace.

5.

Sometimes a Ludicrous Notion

In the airplane back to New York, Steve and I decided that the whole notion was absolutely, positively, unthinkably absurd. $1.7 million! Why not $17 million? Or $170 million? They were all equally preposterous.

How close could we come? So ludicrous was the calculation that we didn't even bother to make it at the time.

If we had, it would have gone something like this: We had an apartment worth, maybe, $500,000 with a $100,000 mortgage. *And that was it!* Except for a few pieces of furniture and some inexpensive artwork, we had *absolutely nothing else!* No stocks, no bonds, no car, no boat, no savings accounts, no IRAs, no trust funds, no indulgent parents, no rich elderly relations (on their deathbeds or elsewhere), no accounts receivable, no real estate developable, no judgments collectible, no jewelry pawnable. The balance in our checking account was pathetic and the prospects for a sudden financial turnaround even worse.

We were, after all, *writers* — not exactly a banker's borrower of choice — just coming off an eight-year project on an advance that amounted to fifty cents an hour (for the pair, not apiece), all of which had long since been spent. Under the circumstances, we weren't even good candidates for a car loan, much less a million-dollar mortgage.

No. It was a ludicrous notion. A nice way to spend a Fourth of July weekend, but nothing more, and we would do ourselves a favor if we forgot all about trying to buy Joye Cottage (ridiculous!) and returned to earth.

The next day, back in New York, we set about the task like demons.

We started by ordering up inspection after inspection and then detailing the depressing results to Wilma Hazlett, in the wild hope, I suppose, that the bleak reports of raining plaster and sagging floors would somehow miraculously cause the seller to throw up his hands in despair and *give* us the keys.

A few phone calls turned up a renovation estimate that a local contractor had prepared years before. It pegged the total cost of fixing the place up at $528,595 — plus, of course, "a 12 percent factor for the contractor's overhead

and profit ($63,431), and a 10 percent contingency allow-
ance ($52,859), for a grand total of $644,885." However,
that figure, the report noted sternly, did *not* include "a new
swimming pool, resurfacing the tennis court, or restoring
and maintaining the grounds around the house."

And even those Brobdingnagian figures — which covered "only the most essential, unfrivolous repairs" — were
pitifully outdated. But in the Alice-in-Wonderland spirit
that marked these efforts, the discovery of this document,
which should have sent us into swoons of discouragement,
was instead the occasion for great celebration and yet another gleefully apocalyptic letter to Wilma.

Next, we set out to prove that no one in his right mind
would want to live in Aiken, South Carolina; the theory
being that, if the community was overvalued, then the
house must be too. The inspiration for this tactic came from
a CBS program on the nuclear weapons industry that aired,
coincidentally, soon after our return from Aiken. Imagine
our surprise to find that this small southern town was home
not only to Joye Cottage but also to the largest nuclear in-
stallation in America, a bomb plant with the suspiciously
self-effacing name "Savannah River Site," which the locals
had further sanitized down to simply SRS.

The CBS show compared SRS with another bomb plant
in Fernald, Ohio, where antinuclear activists had stirred
up a prairie fire of protest that threatened to close the
plant down. While the scenes from Fernald showed angry
mothers anguishing over the high incidence of cancer and
birth defects in their community, the scenes from Aiken
showed a group of good ol' boys sitting around the lobby of

the Ainsley Inn saying that if the stupid people of Fernald wanted to close down their plant, the government was welcome to move it to Aiken.

When we tried to excite Wilma with our fear and indignation over this dizzying display of apathy — this defiant indifference to the possibilities of radioactive leaks and cancer and birth defects — she brushed us aside. "Y'all don't need to worry 'bout that," she said during a phone call one day.

"You mean you trust the *government* to make the plant safe?" I exclaimed in disbelief. "Haven't you seen *China Syndrome?*"

"Lots of people 'round here made a point of *not* seeing that movie," she replied testily.

Later, we discovered that a local real estate developer headed a group called Friends of Nuclear Energy, which worked hard to convince people that nuclear plants made good neighbors and that testing the water in their wells really was unnecessary, even unpatriotic.

Unsatisfied, we called the South Carolina chapter of Greenpeace and asked for their assessment of the risks of living hard by SRS. To our dismay, they said that the daily emission problems in Aiken were a lot less severe than those in a city like, say, Los Angeles, with its necklace of nuclear power plants, and that the water was, in fact, quite safe, since Aiken sat upstream from SRS on the Tuscaloosa aquifer.

"But," we pressed, "what if there is a meltdown? A *China Syndrome?*"

"Everyone within a two-hundred-mile radius would get a lethal dose of radiation," came the answer.

Now, that was more like it.

The man from Greenpeace laughed. "But, of course, that would include Atlanta, Charleston, Savannah, and Charlotte."

SRS may have been endangering the entire southeast quadrant of the United States, but it wasn't going to help us lower the price of Joye Cottage; the threat was too generalized to be of any use to us. In our next letter to Wilma, however, we couldn't resist including the following, rather pathetic warning:

> *Even if SRS doesn't explode or leak radioactive death to surrounding towns like Aiken, surely it is marked in red on Soviet maps and is scheduled for destruction (along with everything nearby) in the first wave of missiles if the unthinkable ever happens.*

Looking back on this campaign, I am struck by the unreality of it all. Nuclear annihilation as a bargaining chip? Why not vaporization discounts? Even if we had been successful in convincing the seller that the price should come down by half a million dollars because the house needed at least that much repair work, *we still couldn't afford it.* And even if we had persuaded him that buying a house within two hundred miles of SRS was like building on quicksand, and, in a paroxysm of guilt, he had cut the price in half, we *still* couldn't afford it. And even if we could, we still couldn't afford the half-million dollars we would need to pay carpenters, plumbers, and roofers to bring the house just up to habitable until the missiles arrived.

But, of course, since we didn't *have* the dollars anyway,

none of that mattered. It was like a game of Monopoly; we were bidding with play money. This was, after all, still the eighties — the *decade* of play money — and like so many Americans at the time, both high rollers and low, we were absolutely determined to buy something that we could not possibly afford.

Until my father arrived.

One month after our initial trip to Aiken, I invited him to join me on a return visit to see the house and to confront, face-to-face for the first time, the seller, a mysterious man whom we knew only as "Mr. Kane."

My *pitch* to Dad was that I needed his expertise. During his fifty years in the hotel business, he had bought and sold more real estate, hired and fired more employees, and taken the measure of more men across more negotiating tables than anyone else I knew. And besides, I didn't have to pay him.

The *truth* was simpler: I was scared.

In the month since we had first made our interest in Joye Cottage known, bits and pieces of information about Mr. Richard Kane had drifted back to us. The portrait they formed was hardly reassuring. An insurance executive from Massachusetts (that's right, a Yankee) with a long list of corporate credentials and very deep pockets, Kane had bought the house from the Whitneys almost a decade before, but never lived in it himself and remained largely aloof from the community. Indeed, much about the man seemed wrapped in rumor. Wilma referred to him as "the stealth seller." But the darkest and most sinister rap on Mr. Kane wasn't rumor at all, it was pure, gut-wrenching fact: He was the man who taught Frank Lorenzo, the infamous union-busting, airline-bankrupting corporate hit man — you guessed it — *how to negotiate!*

The reaction of my father, the hotelier, to the house was predictable: "It would make a great bed-and-breakfast."

"We don't want strangers in our house," I protested.

"If you treat them right, no one's a stranger," he instructed.

No matter how hard I tried, I could not persuade him that two people could live comfortably and inconspicuously in the same space as sixty paying guests. He smiled benignly at my protests and spent most of the afternoon pacing and measuring to assure himself that every bedroom could be accommodated with its own bathroom — a must for a bed-and-breakfast.

A few minutes before we were scheduled to meet with Kane, Dad summoned me to the front steps of Joye Cottage and gravely motioned me to sit down.

"How much can you afford to pay for this house?" he demanded.

After more than a month of mock negotiations and play-money calculations, my father was shining the laser of his common sense into the warm, damp cloud of my fantasy.

"Well . . . I . . . we . . . he wants a million seven for it."

"But how much are you planning to offer?"

"I don't think he'll take less than —"

"Look," he interrupted, "how much do you figure it will cost to fix the place up?" The cloud was dissolving around me, and I didn't like it. When I didn't answer, he prompted, "Well, how much? Surely you've got some estimates."

"Five hundred," I muttered, "maybe six."

"That's way low. It's more like a million. But let's take your figure. Now, how much can you raise?"

"Maybe four hundred thousand from the apartment." Oh, God, the light, the awful light!

"Okay. And how much mortgage can you carry?"

"Another four . . . maybe."

"All right. So you can pull together eight and it'll cost six to fix it up. It's clear then."

"But, but . . . ," I stammered.

Without another word, he got up and headed back to the hotel for the meeting with Kane.

When we knocked at Kane's room, he didn't come to the door; a distant voice bade us enter. Kane was lounging languorously on a peach sofa at the far end of the room. He was a round-faced man with three wavy banners of silver hair, one at the crown and one at each temple, that joined in the back in a downy plume. I had expected a harder look, more angles than curves, more Ivan Boesky than the man behind the curtain in *The Wizard of Oz*.

He didn't get up but held out a beringed hand, palm down, like the pope. My father walked directly up to him and grabbed the proffered hand. My father is not a big man, but he has big, meaty hands, and I thought I detected a wince on Kane's lip as my father pumped the papal hand twice, hard. "Bill Smith."

Kane didn't budge from his power pose: wedged in the corner of the couch with one arm thrown over the back, one foot on the floor and the other propped between the sofa cushions so we could see the sole of his shoe. There were no visible signs of wear on it. A Louis Vuitton suitcase, open but packed and ready to go, was balanced on a luggage rack at the foot of the made bed.

Kane motioned for my father to take a large, prehensile wing chair at the far end of the room. My father ignored his directions, grabbed a straight-backed desk chair, and set it down firmly only a few feet from Kane's sofa. When he sat down and crossed his legs, their shoes almost touched: Dad's ancient wingtip and Kane's unblemished loafer. Kane tugged at his Bermuda-green polo shirt in discomfort. I took the most marginal seat in the room, a dressing stool next to the open-jawed suitcase.

I remember the scene well: the Pasha Kane, Maharajah of Joye Cottage, reclining lazily on his divan; my father, Willy Loman, leaning forward, elbows on knees, all concentration and energy; and me, all raw nerve ends. I remember less well the conversation — except that it was very brief.

"You know we're talking about a unique property?" Kane began. He spoke only to my father, assuming, mistakenly, that the money would come from the only other man in the room with gray hair.

"All the harder to put a value on," my father countered. "I hear it's been on the market for some time — years, in fact."

"We've been waiting for the right price."

"There's no such thing," my father corrected, with a chiding chuckle. "We both know that. It's worth what you can get for it."

Kane's eyes narrowed mirthlessly. "I certainly don't intend to lose money on it."

"Of course not," my father said, still chuckling, enjoying himself. "No one ever *intends* to lose money. But we're both realists. We know that some deals make money, and some deals lose money. Good deals, bad deals."

"I don't make bad deals."

"Every businessman makes a bad deal now and then."

"Not this one," Kane deadpanned. "What's your offer, Mr. Smith? You *do* have an offer?"

My father leaned forward on his elbows. "We figure the property's worth eight hundred thousand . . ."

Kane, impatiently: "The offer?"

". . . fixed up."

"The offer?"

"And it will take at least six hundred to fix up . . ."

"The offer . . . ?"

"Two hundred thousand. It's a fair offer."

There it was. Even as the dream of Joye Cottage collapsed, I had to admire my father's *cojones*. Two hundred thousand dollars! One *tenth* the asking price. *"It's a fair offer!"*

Without a word, Kane sprang from his peach sofa, grabbed his suitcase, slammed it shut like a giant book, and strode from the room on his virgin loafers. At the door, he turned to say, "I don't believe we have any further business to discuss," then disappeared.

That was it. Months of fantasizing undone in five minutes of bargaining. On the ride back to the airport, I wanted to stop by the house one last time, but my father talked me out of it. "You'll find something you like even better," he kept saying. "All you have to do is look."

6.

Joye Cottage *sur Mer*

God, did we look.

Returning to Sotheby's, where the madness began, we looked at grand estates on the Long Island shore, horse farms in Virginia, genuine historic landmarks in Mississippi, and private islands out of Ian Fleming in the Bahamas. After months of picturing the green vistas and sunlit verandas of Joye Cottage, we had developed a virtual horror of remaining in New York, and driven by that horror, we looked everywhere: South Carolina, North Carolina, Georgia, Virginia, Florida, Mississippi, Louisiana, Texas, Kansas, Arizona, Maryland, Delaware, upstate New York, downstate New York, Jamaica, the Virgin Islands, Ireland, Italy. We looked at every price: from $300,000 for a farmhouse in New Jersey to $30,000,000 for an eighteenth-century palace near Lisbon. We looked at every style: from postmodern antebellum in Alabama, to robber baronial in Washington State, to ancestral decrepit in Maine.

We looked and looked until finally we ended up where we could find all of these houses at all of these prices in all of these styles within a few feet of each other: Malibu, California.

Three months to the day after Kane stomped out of his hotel room on that steamy Sunday in South Carolina, Steve and I stood on a windswept hilltop overlooking the Pacific Ocean. The sun was a perfect yellow, the hills a perfect gold, the sea a perfect blue. White cottony puffs of clouds above and green frondy clumps of trees below, placed in perfect randomness, as if by some Hollywood set designer. The ocean, lying in gilded longueurs between the hills, was truly, heartstoppingly beautiful.

Our guide, driver, and real-estate-agent-of-the-moment, Dawn Julie, squinted into the sunlight through her black-black, nearly opaque sunglasses. "It's got to be around here somewhere," she chirped, then buried her pretty blond head back in the map, confirming what Steve and I had suspected for the last few miles of hairpin canyon turns and breathtaking scenery: We were lost.

The moment was rich with irony.

We had come to Los Angeles originally to meet with our agent at William Morris to discuss selling the movie rights to our still-unpublished Pollock biography. But Joye Cottage lingered in our thoughts like an unrequited love, and as soon as the meetings were done, we scheduled a day of house hunting. One day led to two, and so it went. We looked at houses on stilts, balanced like spinning plates, in the Hollywood Hills; we looked at Bela Lugosi's house, nestled within the contrived tropical foliage of Beverly Hills; we looked at million-dollar country cottages in Pasadena, million-and-a-half-dollar bungalows in Bel Air, and two-million-dollar shacks by the sea in Malibu. This was, after all, the height of the California real estate boom (later bubble), when in some neighborhoods, a million dollars bought you exactly five rooms, a driveway, a pool, and an address — if you got a deal.

But no matter how expensive the house, how famous its former occupant, how prestigious its address, or how spectacular its views, nothing we saw measured up to Joye Cottage. If Joye Cottage, with all its grand rooms and colonnaded verandas, could be somehow magically transported from the pine barrens of South Carolina to the palm valleys of southern California, we wondered, how much would it be worth? What would the asking price be? Ten times what Richard Kane was asking? Twenty times? Not surprisingly, this calculation did little to cheer us up.

Unable to find a house to match the image in our heads — even after several more cross-country trips — and intoxicated by the views of the Pacific Ocean from the Malibu hills, we conceived a new and, in retrospect, even more preposterous plan: We would *build* our dream house.

And who better to design it than my cousin Bub, he of the vast learning and exquisite sensibilities, who had moved on from the sand villas of our youth to become an architect of real buildings in New York City. In designing a seaside

Malibu home for Steve and me, Bub, who now preferred the first name "Robert" and the last name "Rich & Associates," reached back into our cattle-cut days and captured the magic of those doomed Roman extravaganzas. It was a magnificent design, with a classical facade and a grand inner courtyard that stepped down, parterre by parterre, so that the long colonnaded arms on either side reached out and embraced a breathtaking view of the green hills and blue Pacific. It was thrilling. It was perfect. It was, in fact, Joye Cottage *sur mer!*

The only question (other than money, which we were practiced at not thinking about) was where to put it. Thus did our quest for the perfect house become a quest for the perfect piece of land. And it was that quest that had brought us to the windswept heights of Latigo Canyon Road in the red convertible and strange company of the girl-woman with two first names, Dawn Julie.

"I think it's either that hilltop," she said, lowering her sunglasses back into place with one hand and pointing with the other, "or that one." She looked at her map again and then back at the horizon; the sunglasses moved up and down. "Or that one." She may not have been able to read a map, but what she was doing with those sunglasses was high art. Like motorized louvers, they swung up and down on the pivot of her ears, one minute acting as hairband for her long, sunstreaked locks, the next minute lowering to cover the puzzled look in her eyes as she surveyed the hilltops nearby, searching for the two acres of scrub that corresponded to 5906 Latigo Canyon Road on her map.

Eventually, she gave up. "I know it's *one* of these hill-tops," she concluded, sweeping her arm along a 270-degree

arc of vista that included most of Malibu and all of the Pacific Ocean. "We can always figure out which one later."
She seemed satisfied with that. "What really matters," she
reminded us, "is the view."

When, after much searching, we finally found the flags
that marked the boundaries of 5906, we realized that this
particular hilltop lot was all hill and no top. To put Robert's
sprawling villa on this lot would be roughly the equivalent
of setting a banquet table on the tip of an intercontinental
ballistic missile.

And about as safe. "What about fires?" Steve asked when
he saw a pile of charred bricks on a neighboring lot. "I've
heard they have a lot of grass fires around here."

No problem, Dawn assured us. "The fire-prone areas are
up there, and over there," she said, pointing north and east.

"And the pile of charred bricks?"

"Maybe somebody's barbecue."

Unreassured, we asked to stop and talk to the nearest neighbor. When we knocked, a silver-haired lady in a turquoise sweatsuit came to the door. What is that pile of charred bricks next door? we asked. Was there a house there? "Oh, yes," she answered brightly. "There have been three houses there. All of them burned down." (Later, we discovered that to build on 5906, we would have to get fire department approval, and to do that we would have to pay for a water tank, a pump, a sprinkler system, and a 600-foot well, at a total estimated cost of $34,300. In addition, we would have to pay for improvements to the access road so that fire trucks could *get* to 5906, which they currently could not, which explained the pile of charred bricks. That would be another $50,000, maybe more.)

I tried to explain to Dawn Julie that we already had a design for our house, that we needed at least one acre of *flat* ground to put it on, and that 5906 had barely a square foot of flat ground. "No problem," she said. "Just bring in some fill. They're building malls all around this area." She obviously considered this exceedingly good news, as well as the solution to our problem with 5906. "And they're always looking for ways to get rid of the dirt."

But what about earthquakes and mudslides? Wasn't fill especially vulnerable?

"You can do what the L.A. County Museum does," she suggested helpfully. "You can put everything on rollers."

"Why don't we just put the whole *house* on rollers?" Steve mocked.

"That would work, too," she bubbled.

Sensing our interest in 5906 waning, Dawn tried petu-

lance. "You know, of course, that Michael Landon is building a house right down there," she said, pointing over the
single square foot of flat ground toward the valley on the
other side. Sure enough, in a lush green, tree-filled hollow
just beyond and a few hundred feet below 5906, a huge
concrete-shelled house was rising. Construction was far
enough along that you could make out an inner courtyard
ringed with arches. The Spanish red-tile roof lay half on,
half on pallets. "He's building his own little house on the
prairie," said Dawn in her Valley Girl voice, with a toss of
her golden hair. "There are people who would die to get this
close to a star."

That, we decided, was precisely what anybody who built
on 5906 would do.

Malibu marked not only land's end, but also the end of
our search. Having swept the entire nation in search of a
place to live, we had simply run out of continent. We continued to look, of course, in a desultory way, as pictures of
houses around the country continued to trickle in from real
estate agents we had met on our quest: a Victorian town-
house in San Francisco, a funeral home in Charleston, an
adobe ranch in Santa Fe. But our hearts weren't in it.

Over the next six months, only one prospect excited us:
the former governor's mansion in my old hometown,
Columbus — a grand Beaux-Arts brick and limestone affair. But we were interested in it only if we could disassem-
ble it brick by brick and *move it to Malibu* — an idea that, in
retrospect, set new standards of impracticality and point-
lessness. If we felt like rejected suitors, this was the equivalent of flinging ourselves off a cliff.

Then one day, out of the blue, we received a letter:

... I am sorry that our last encounter ended so abruptly. In the months since, I have had a chance to reconsider your offer and I would be interested in resuming negotiations regarding your purchase of the property known as Joye Cottage.

Richard Kane

When I read my father the letter, he said it sounded like capitulation to him.

It was.

To this day, we have never known for sure why Richard Kane, the Donald Trump of Easy Street, the man who "never made a bad deal," came back to the bargaining table. At the time, we were too flabbergasted to ask, and neither Wilma nor, certainly, Kane ever offered an explanation. Over the months of negotiations that followed, however, and in bits and pieces of information that floated back to us from time to time afterward, we learned enough to make a pretty good guess.

If Joye Cottage was our dream house, it was Richard Kane's house of horrors. Our Easy Street, his Elm Street. In buying the place, Kane had fought with the Whitneys over price, over contents, over inspections, over dates, over conditions, and especially over money. "Mr. Kane was finally brought to bay," one member of the Whitney family complained at the time. "The deal is over and done with, and if I never hear the name Kane again, it will be too soon for me."

Kane's first plan was to convert the house into "an executive conference center." He published glossy brochures for prospective "investor/owners" touting "the tax benefits of ownership" in such an historic property. When these calls met with deafening silence, the plan changed. Instead of executive suites, he would transform the house into an *exclusive* private club with "a number of residential suites available to members." When that plan, too, foundered, Kane tried filling the house with rich retired northerners in an *exclusive* retirement community. Finally, in desperation, he had plans drawn up to chop the place into half a dozen *exclusive* condominiums.

One by one, however, neighbors and city officials torpedoed the variances and permits Kane needed to float his grand, *exclusive* schemes, and as they did, the price of splendor began to drop. In the end, we bought Joye Cottage for less than we got for our two-bedroom, sunless apartment with the postage-stamp park view. Twenty thousand square feet for less than the price of eighteen hundred.

Location, location, location.

After so much agony, the end came with stunning swiftness: agreement, signing, closing, key.

The house was ours.

7.

Good-bye, Manhattan

Our last night in New York, we went to a party given by a friend in the building. She lives in a grand terraced duplex in the towers overlooking the park and the reservoir, with heartstopping views of the Manhattan skyline. While it's true that her apartment and ours shared the same building, it's also true that the chicken and the eagle are both birds.

Esther Feinberg is a well-known collector of modern art, and on the walls throughout her apartment, between the windows filled with spectacular panoramas of Manhattan by night, hung paintings that simply took your breath away:

Picasso, Matisse, Kandinsky, Léger, Mondrian, even Pollock. And all of a quality that any museum in the world
would envy. All this and food too. It was the best New York
had to offer.

The party had been planned for months, and we weren't
even the guests of honor, but coming as it did on the eve of
our departure, Steve and I treated it like a going-away bash.
Between mouthfuls of salmon dip and tiramisu, we told war
stories, common at the time, about our six-month ordeal in
the New York real estate market. Everyone in the room
knew the market had taken a turn south, but *we* knew exactly
how far south. We had been there. Within the first month
after we put our apartment on the market, real estate agents
lowered their appraisal by $100,000, then by $200,000. And
the same thing was happening all over New York. Never had
so much been lost by so many who had so little in the first
place.

For the first few weeks, we saw more agents than clients,
a parade of agents inexplicably desperate to add our sad,
sunless apartment to their already long lists of unsold prop-
erties. All with identical worried, sympathetic expressions,
like hospital visitors, they would pace the apartment
muttering encouraging blandishments: "How charming!"
"What a great old building!" "I love the lobby!" "Isn't this
an ingenious layout!" "So much closet space!" Then, when
an offer came in at half the asking price, "You know, it *is* a
small apartment." "It really *is* too dark." "It would help if
there was a *real* view." "This floor plan *is* hard to work
with." "But it doesn't *feel* like two thousand square feet."

We recounted our pathetic efforts to make the apartment

more sellable, which amounted to disguising its flaws without openly lying about them. To prove it was sunnier than it looked (as in Mark Twain's comment that Wagner's music is "better than it sounds"), we waited until a day in midsummer when, because of the alignment of the sun, the earth, and nearby buildings, a shaft of sunlight blundered through our living room windows. This natural phenomenon, akin to the yearly astronomical alignments at Stonehenge, occurred for only about five days every summer, but we captured it on film and left the pictures conspicuously on a table to show prospective buyers.

Every time a buyer arrived at the front desk, we ran downstairs to the concert pianist who lived below us and pleaded, cajoled, and bullied her into taking an intermission. "It must be very quiet living here at the back of the building," a buyer would say. "Like living in the country," we would say, nodding our heads (knowing that, at times, it was more like living over the stage at Carnegie Hall).

It took our agent six months, but she did eventually unload our "chicken," and for a price that, while less than we originally hoped, was still more than twice what we had paid five years earlier. That she sold it at all, given the ruinous state of the market, was miraculous. Based on the stories we were hearing, we decided that ours had to be *the last* apartment sold in New York City in 1989.

The other guests listened in rapt attention to our tales, anxiously inferring from our ordeal how they and their apartments might fare *in* similar *extremis*. We were like old sailors returned from a voyage to the antipodes with accounts of new worlds, alien tribes, and strange rituals. They listened with the pricked ears of fellow sailors who knew they might someday have to navigate the same perilous seas.

Then they heard that we were sailing *back*, to a place far *beyond* the antipodes, to the most distant and alien place imaginable: South Carolina.

"You're moving *where?*" exclaimed a woman in a perfect Chanel suit. We explained that Aiken was roughly halfway between Columbia, South Carolina, and Augusta, Georgia. Her look of puzzled anticipation didn't change. We explained that Augusta was about two hours east of Atlanta. That name elicited recognition and a new concern: "But where will you *eat?*"

As the word spread among the guests that two of their number were moving to the deepest South, heads periscoped above the crowd. Where were these intrepid explorers? Everyone we met, like the lady in the Chanel suit, wanted to know *why*, to fathom this strange and marvelous news.

"So, what's the theater like in Atlanta?" asked a psychiatrist who could barely restrain himself from offering to help cure us of this bizarre mental dysfunction. "They have a ballet, don't they?" "Do you think you'll find enough to *do* down there?" asked the piano player from downstairs whom we had muzzled so often. "Who on Earth will you *talk* to?" our hostess wondered. The caterers looked at us sadly.

In the end, though, they were all expressing the same sentiment: My God, you're stepping off the end of the earth!

When we had told all our stories and answered all their questions, and the party began to break up, Steve and I slipped out a side door and onto the terrace to catch one final glimpse of the Manhattan skyline by night.

It was even more splendorous than I remembered.

When I came to New York ten years earlier and saw that skyline for the first time — not as a poster, or a postcard, or the background in a Woody Allen film, but as a *home* — I remember thinking, sitting in our second-floor apartment, that I could feel all those people piled around me and on top of me like so many millions of bricks in a vast fortress of humanity. And wondering how I could ever think of my little space among so many as a home.

But now, sitting on the dark terrace looking back through the windows into the amber-lit room filled with fellow New Yorkers, thinking that within a few days I would be gone, on to another home, suddenly the great power of familiarity asserted itself.

When I was a child, we moved twice before ending up on Fair Avenue (not often by most people's standards, and positively stationary compared to Steve's family's forty-eight moves). Each time, on moving day, I would maneuver around my parents and the movers to ensure that I was the last person to leave the house. In that final moment, with my mother calling for me from the crammed station wagon in the driveway, I would stand near a wall, lay my small, pudgy palms against it, lean ceremoniously forward on my pudgy toes, and kiss the old house good-bye.

No, I didn't plant a kiss on the grimy sandstone walls of

the El Dorado that night. But I thought about it. And on the eve of leaving for South Carolina and Joye Cottage, I thought about how memories, not bricks or boards, make a house, and how you always feel like a stranger for a while in a new one, no matter how old it is, surrounded by other people's pasts.

Part Two A Big Job

8.

Moving Out

Almost exactly one year after our first sight of Joye Cottage, we stood on the veranda, surveying the sun-washed porches, the eternity of leaves, the virgin white clapboard surrounded by jade-green lawns, and realized it all belonged to us.

And the bank.

Before we could move in, however, we had to move *out*. Paradoxically, decades of emptiness had left the house filled to bursting. The main rooms were vacant enough, except for the odd chair or table, lonely survivors of the repeated rummage sales Mr. Kane staged in a desperate and ultimately doomed battle to derail the juggernaut of bad judgment.

But just beyond the big empty rooms, out of sight of the casual visitor, was a wilderness of junk. In the closets, in the attics, in the basements where there were basements, in the crawlspaces where there weren't, lay a century of discards: the stuff deemed unwanted or unneeded not just once, but again and again, as successive occupants discovered and discarded it, pushing it farther and farther into obscurity to make room for the newest discards.

Closets, all forty-five of them, became archaeological digs. In one, the bottom drawer contained screwdrivers, brass hinges, and pieces of a broken latch-box wrapped in a parchmentlike piece of newspaper indicating that this closet had recently been used as a makeshift toolshed. Farther up, on the side of another drawer an old, yellowed label read "petticoats," indicating an earlier, more domestic use. At the back of a high shelf was a little box, shrouded in dust, and in it, a tiny stuffed tiger, limp and pale, a gold garnet ring for a tiny finger, and a perfume bottle in the shape of a Scottie dog. It wasn't hard to imagine some Whitney child carefully storing her most precious Carolina things as she headed off to school somewhere up north, pledging to return someday. When we moved the box, it left a square of gleaming wood where a speck of dust hadn't fallen since Teddy Roosevelt lived and breathed.

The basements, all four of them, were so full that the doors wouldn't open, so full we couldn't imagine how the last items were added. Were the basements sealed from the inside? Did the owners of Joye Cottage, like the ancient pharaohs, bury their minions alongside their worldly goods to guard them in the afterlife? When we beat down the old rotten doors, we found, not the bones of the faithful, but a stack of furniture fallen over when the legs on the bottommost rotted through and collapsed.

▲

To perform the Herculean task of cleaning out this hundred years' accumulation, we hired a crew of "laborers," the local term for unskilled day workers who would do almost anything for $4.50 an hour. All the laborers were black — not just the ones we hired, but *all* the men, young and old, who gathered every morning at six in the dewy yard of a local building-supply company hoping for the chance to do a hard day's work in exchange for less than the cost of fixing a single broken window in New York.

The "captain" of our crew was Mordia Grant, a twenty-six-year-old husband and father who, at five feet, five inches and one hundred pounds, looked more like a teenager than a work-gang boss. Mordia came by his unofficial leadership position not by strength or smarts — although he was, indeed, very smart — but by *style.* Dressed in jade-green silk sweatpants and purple silk shirt, one discreet gold earring, and a haircut like the front end of a vintage car — fins and side grills with a magnificent blond streak for a hood ornament — Mordia ruled by the hard law of hipness. (Eventually, he gave similar haircuts to all the other laborers on the project, turning his crew into a kind of kinetic sculpture garden, all angles and curves and squiggles and stripes. He called it Top Art.)

Curious name, Mordia. We wondered where he got it.

"From my mother," he deadpanned.

Did he know what the name meant?

"No."

Death.

"No. You gotta be shittin' me."

It's true. Mortician, mortuary, mordant . . . Mordia.

Mordia looked genuinely stung by this alarming news. "Well," he sputtered, "I might as well just hang it up."

During just the first week of work, Mordia and his gang hauled out of the darkness and into the sunlight a mountain of discards: rotten lengths of fencing and gates, carpets that the moths had long since gagged on, furniture that had fallen into unrecognizable fragments, crippled and muti- lated screen doors, dismembered radiators, rusty garden implements, a mangled push mower like a piece of modern sculpture, a five-ton boiler, two tons of coal, a three-hundred- gallon hot-water tank, hundreds of feet of iron piping from the old boiler system, miles of old wire, and one thirty-foot telephone pole.

And what did we do with all that pharaonic trash? (You can't put a five-ton boiler in the garbage can for Tuesday pick-up.)

Simple. We gave it to Lucky.

9.

The Grand Acquisitor

Lucky Dale advertised himself as a chimney sweep, and it was in that Dickensian role that he made his debut at Joye Cottage.

And what a debut it was.

Standing in the doorway, tall and statuesque, bearded and dressed entirely in black, from his boots to his stovepipe hat, he looked like a cross between Abraham Lincoln and an extra from *Mary Poppins*. It wasn't until later I learned that his mentors at the chimney sweep school in Massachusetts where he trained were so impressed by his bearded, Rushmore features topped by a stovepipe hat that they adopted his profile as their school logo. He looked born to the trade. (In fact, he had worked in a grocery store until the age of thirty-three, a late start in the sweep business.)

For the next three weeks, Lucky arrived every morning in a rattly old van emblazoned on every side with his distinctive silhouette. From his front bumper dangled a battered stovepipe hat, which he considered the symbol of his trade. No matter how early he arrived, his face was always black with soot. I imagined his wife, an ample woman who sometimes worked with him, carefully applying the soot with a blush brush every morning just before Lucky jumped in his van and drove off to work. When he arrived, his sons would clamber down from the van like street urchins out of *Oliver Twist*. They all had names like June Bug, Moon Dog, and Pip, and were all as long and lanky as Lucky himself.

With this improbable crew, Lucky went to work gutting chimneys, relining flues, rebuilding fireboxes — and sweeping — all in the grimmest, grimiest of conditions. With twenty-six fireplaces in thirteen chimneys, some crumbling and none with dampers (meaning most of our heat was going, literally, up in smoke), we needed *a lot* of chimney work.

But Lucky's greatest service to Joye Cottage wasn't in our chimneys; it was in our trash heap. For Lucky Dale was more than just the poster boy of chimney sweeps, he was the king of pack rats. If the Nobel committee were ever to give a prize for recycling, Lucky would be a shoo-in to stride across the stage in Oslo and shake King Olaf's hand.

No matter what we threw away, Lucky had a use for it.

The old telephone pole — he sawed it into beams that he used for roof supports in a shed he was building. The old boiler — broken apart and sold as scrap metal for a few pennies a pound. The old galvanized iron pipes that we were replacing with copper — cut up and used for fence posts. Was there *anything* he couldn't reuse? "What's the strangest thing you've ever salvaged?" Steve asked one day as Lucky walked out of the house with a wild spool of ancient, lead-coated wire.

Lucky pondered for a while, then said, in his flawless, educated English (he occasionally brought his poetry for us to review): "I guess that would have to be a forty-foot concrete grain silo I took from an old lady in Beech Island. I traded it for a fifty-dollar cleaning of her chimney."

And what new use did he find for a forty-foot concrete grain silo?

"I made an apartment out of it," said Lucky. A *three-story* apartment, he explained, with a combination kitchen-dining room on the first floor, a living room on the second floor, a bedroom on the third floor, and a spiral staircase connecting them. "It was supposed to be a guest cottage, but my wife and I stay up there a lot ourselves," he confessed. "It's unique."

But the silo was just the tip of the iceberg, so to speak. For Lucky, it turned out, was the grand acquisitor of all time. Not just the king of pack rats, the *Sun King* of collectors. His collection of phonograph records, for example, totaled 1.2 million discs, all bought at yard sales, flea markets, and estate sales for practically nothing (e.g., 5,000 records for $150), and included everything from classical to rockabilly to rap. To play this vast collection of records, he kept a vast collection of record players: players for 45s and 78s; ancient phonographs for the fifteen-inch transcriptions used by radio stations in the thirties; even players for little round cylinders, of which he had almost 2,500.

But records were just the beginning. His collection of 350,000 magazines included full sets of *Life, Look,* the *Saturday Evening Post,* and *National Geographic,* as well as long-out-of-print rarities like *Women's Home Companion* and *Pictorial Review.* And then there were the newspapers: virtually every issue of every paper in the region, some of them going back a hundred years or more.

Then there were the postcards (more than twenty thousand of them) and the View Master cards (twenty thousand of them, too; the world's largest collection). Just weeks before, Lucky had stumbled upon a copy of the *first* View Master card ever made (by Sawyer's in Portland, Oregon, in the late 1920s) on sale at a flea market for fifty cents.

"The seller had no idea what the thing was," said Lucky, "but I knew right away."

Then, finally, there were the dolls. That's right, dolls. Lucky Dale Meissinger, all soot-covered, chimney-sweeping six-plus feet of him, was a doll collector, an obsession he inherited from *both* parents. His mother, a renowned authority on Shirley Temple dolls, of which she owned more than six hundred, sat on the board of directors of the Shirley Temple Doll Club. His father, also an STDC board member, had just recently stepped down as president of the Madam Alexander Doll Club. The Meissinger seniors' largest holdings, in fact, were in Madam Alexander dolls. "One person's trash is another's treasure," the elder Lucky often told his son.

To house his vast, varied, and growing collections, Lucky had built his personal Xanadu on a rolling piece of farmland between Aiken and Augusta. Hearst-like, he started with a modest nine-hundred-square-foot A-frame and added to it, and added and added, until he had more than twenty thousand square feet of temperature- and humidity-controlled warehouse space — exactly what we had in Joye Cottage.

"We call the place Connemara," Lucky told us. "That's an Irish word, and it means 'refuge from a troubled world.'"

10.

The Whitney Silver

While Lucky and Mordia did their dirty work, Steve and I moved into Joye Cottage's squash courts, one of the original estate's outbuildings that had been sold off during the 1950s and converted into a handsome, spacious home in its own right. The owner, a seasonal resident, had graciously invited us to stay there until we could make a place to sleep in our huge, uninhabitable hovel.

Desperate to snatch a few rooms from the jaws of decrepitude before the winter set in, we hired more and more laborers. Soon there were a dozen, spread thin over sixty rooms and five acres — more than we could possibly keep an eye on.

That was our first mistake.

One day I walked out back to check on the progress of weeding the tennis court and repainting the fence that surrounded it. Knowing that this job lay far from our regular patrol paths, Steve and I had assigned it to Jeff Watson, a laborer whose apparent energy and reliability had catapulted him overnight to the top of the labor-pool ladder, just a rung below Mordia. But still, it didn't hurt to check.

There was Jeff, sitting on the brick steps leading to the tennis court, in the speckled shade of a rust-leafed dogwood tree. He was leaning on his elbows, head back, eyes closed. His feet twitched in complex accompaniment as Whitney Houston's voice rolled across the lawn from the radio in his car, which he had parked on the street strategically near the tennis court with its windows down. The music filled the neighborhood.

The weeds and fence, of course, were untouched.

The music was so loud he didn't hear my approach. I was about ten feet away, no more, when he finally opened his eyes, saw me, and leapt to his feet.

"Why were you sitting down?" I demanded.

"I wasn't sitting down," he said.

"What do you mean, you weren't sitting down?"

"I wasn't sitting down," he insisted.

"What do you mean, you weren't sitting down?" I insisted. "I just *saw* you sitting down."

"That wasn't me," he insisted.

So you can imagine our surprise when we arrived at the

house one morning early — before work was even supposed to begin — and found Mordia and his crew, including Jeff, furiously digging in a crawlspace that had been cleaned out the previous week. Mordia laughed nervously when we demanded to know what was going on. Finally, he pulled us aside, out of hearing of the others, and whispered, "It's the silver. You know, the Widney Silver."

It wasn't the first we had heard of the fabled Whitney Silver. I don't remember when or how the rumor reached us, but it didn't take long. "You know, there's silver in that house," some total stranger confided. "Millions of dollars' worth!" No one had specifics, of course, except to say that the Whitneys were fabulously wealthy and were known for their magnificent silver collection. Why the Whitneys, who were clever enough to make all that money, had absent-mindedly left Joye Cottage without taking their silver with them — millions of dollars' worth, no less — was never explained. "It's hidden in there *somewhere*," a waitress at Shoney's told us with the utter conviction of the utterly uninformed.

"Somewhere," of course, wasn't much help in a house with sixty rooms. Inevitably, the workers' attention, and ours, was drawn to two areas of the house that had resisted all efforts at exploration. The first was a large, brick-walled vault in the basement directly under the front-porch steps. Judging from the exterior dimensions, the room inside had to be at least ten by twelve feet, more than enough for the missing hoard. The door, a massive, antique steel contraption of the kind Bonnie and Clyde must have encountered, bore the scars of generations of vandals and, undoubtedly, silver

prospectors. We found a rusty sledgehammer with a splintered handle lying at its foot.

Similarly defiant was a big floor safe that sat on a concrete pad in one of the underground passageways connecting the wings of the house. These dark, low-ceilinged passageways, with their crumbling plaster walls and old walk boards, formed a kind of domestic catacomb that allowed maids and butlers to move unseen from wing to wing. A big black block of steel the size of a refrigerator, the floor safe came to our attention long before silver fever struck the work site, but for a different reason: We needed to move it. Sitting as it did astride a main thoroughfare that ran from one end of the house to the other, like so much else, it had to go. But where? How? When we sent six of our strongest laborers to inch it toward the nearest stairway, it moved not a micron.

One morning, we arrived at the house and found the safe open. Mordia informed us that one of the laborers — he said he didn't know which one — had come early and successfully cracked the lock. "But don't worry," Mordia assured us, "cracking a safe isn't like picking a house lock." Somehow, we found that less than comforting. By the time we arrived, of course, the safe was empty, although Mordia also assured us that it was found in that condition by the opener — "whoever he was."

The vault, apparently, resisted similar efforts, which left us with two mysteries: What was in the vault, and how to move the safe?

11.

The Information Highway

As we watched the workers tear the house apart, shining their flashlights into every crack and crevice, squirming into every sliver of crawlspace, peering into every attic and kneewall, probing up every chimney and digging test holes wherever they could sink a shovel, all with an animation and energy never brought to their paid duties, Steve and I wondered how stupid rumors like the one about the Whitney Silver ever get started in the first place.

That was before we met Frank Hatch.

Frank was Aiken's answer to all those friends in New York who, upon hearing that we were moving to a small town in South Carolina, got this stricken look on their faces and asked in the most plaintive voices, *"But who will cut your hair!!??* No one in a town that small cuts hair properly."* One especially gloomy prophet told us about a couple she knew who moved to faraway Ohio but had to return to Manhattan *every six weeks* for forty-dollar shearings on Madison Avenue.

One thing and only one thing about that prophecy turned out to be true: We would *never* be able to pay forty dollars for a haircut in Aiken, South Carolina. The rest was a false alarm.

Frank Hatch ran his one-chair shop in a little violet-painted brick building in "downtown" Aiken. The shop was called simply Frank's (like Kenneth's). Young, short, with close-cropped curly hair and an innocent, amiable face, Frank may have been a notch or two below Kenneth in the tonsorial pecking order, but he wasn't the Main Street barber in Bexley, Ohio, either. And the price? A very un–New York fourteen dollars.

And that fourteen dollars entitled you to much more than a wash, cut, and style. It was, in fact, a toll — a toll that gave you unlimited access to Aiken's version of the information highway. From the time you walked in the door and sat down behind a table laden with *Mademoiselle* and *International Male,* the gossip was as thick as Strom Thurmond's accent. Nothing escaped Frank's hearing, and anything that went in his ear sooner or later came out his mouth.

One day, early on, I made the mistake of asking Frank if he knew anything about our neighbors. For the next hour, I heard vividly detailed accounts of the nymphomaniacal former B-movie actress who exposed herself every morning to the stable hands from her bedroom window; of the wayward heir to a vast fortune who happened to be both a sleepwalker and an inveterate gambler; of the local "duchess" who was really a former department store clerk. And all for only fourteen dollars.

But that was nothing compared to the scoop that Frank dropped on Steve one day. "Have you heard that Madonna was in town?"

"Madonna?" Steve's brain strained to merge the images of writhing bodies from "Express Yourself" and the portly matrons who ran the handicraft booths at the "Aiken's Makin'" festival.

"Madonna?"

"Yeah," Frank said with absolute certainty. "She's looking for a house in Aiken."

How did he know?

"The agent who showed her around told me. She swore me to secrecy, of course."

Of course.

On our first visit to Aiken, we had heard a rumor (not from Frank) that Sylvester Stallone had shown some interest in Joye Cottage at one time. And crooner Andy Williams had, in fact, once owned the old W. R. Grace estate, Two Trees. But *Madonna?* In *Aiken?* Why, we wondered, would a fabulously rich self-made superstar, a fashion-setting, scandal-baiting, convention-breaking, sexual omnivore come to Aiken, South Carolina?

Then we realized: Such a person had *already* come to Aiken.

And built Joye Cottage.

12.

Material Boy

Ever since discovering our rambling wreck, we had been eager to find out more about the man who built it: William Collins Whitney, known to his friends as "W.C." The Sotheby's brochure referred to him only as a "celebrated entrepreneur and former Secretary of the Navy." Local lore painted him more colorfully, but no more helpfully, as an eccentric zillionaire with a towering edifice complex (in addition to Joye Cottage, the town boasted polo fields, stables, an indoor tennis court, a golf club, and a twelve-hundred-acre forest, all of which were either built with Whitney money, given by Whitney, named after Whitney, or all of the above). Once we started work on the house, and all its idiosyncrasies and secrets began to emerge, so did a clearer portrait of its creator.

He was the gilding on the Gilded Age. When he threw his great "New Century's Eve" party on December 31, 1899, William C. Whitney was not only one of the most famous and popular men in America, he was the undisputed king of New York society. They called him "Mr. Fifth Avenue," after the most exclusive street in the most fashionable city in the richest country in the world. Whitney owned not one, not two, but three houses on *the* Avenue, and he could be seen almost every morning — when he wasn't in Washington running the country or sailing the oceans on his 206-foot yacht — strolling its sidewalks in chamois gloves and top hat.

And when *he* walked the Avenue, people noticed. Six foot one, handsome as a Greek god, and always impeccably tailored, Whitney turned heads wherever he went. Women found him irresistible: some for his millions, some for his power, and some for his big, blue-gray bedroom eyes.

At parties, he could discourse knowledgeably on everything from politics and business to music and art to horses and golf — a vital skill, what with eight-course dinners, and balls, and banquets three or four nights a week. He was a superb horseman, it was said, who drove a coach "as Ben-Hur drove a chariot." He even had a good singing voice.

In a city filled with parvenus and pretenders, W.C. was a true blue blood. Massachusetts Bay Colony on his father's side, Plymouth Colony on his mother's. A real Mayflower heritage. The right schools, of course — Yale for college,

Harvard for law school — where he played the right sport, crew, and joined the right "society," Skull and Bones, of course. So impeccable were his credentials that when he arrived in New York, no club could turn him away: Union, Knickerbocker, Century, University, Manhattan, Metropolitan, Jockey, Yacht, Mayflower, Meadow Brook, Racquet and Tennis — he belonged to them all. It was said he could eat at one of his clubs every day for three weeks without repeating himself.

The right roots, right schools, and right clubs, of course, translated into the right friends. Elihu Root was his lawyer; the Vanderbilts, his next-door neighbors. His circle included Thomas Fortune Ryan, J. Pierpont Morgan, William Rockefeller, Andrew Carnegie, Joseph Widener, Whitelaw Reid, Stuyvesant Fish, Isabella Stewart Gardner, Joseph Pulitzer. With friends like that, how could Mrs. Astor and Ward McAllister *not* invite him to their famous ball? He wasn't just one of the four hundred, he was one of the forty. One of the four!

But, as all the doormen at New York's hottest nightspots knew, there was much more to W.C. than blue blood and greenbacks.

With the possible exception of Mrs. Astor's ballroom, the heart of W.C.'s New York society was at Fifth and 44th. On the northeast corner was Delmonico's, the oldest and most fashionable restaurant in town, a place where dinner was "not merely an ingestion, but an observance." Next door, at Richard Canfield's sumptuous gambling establishment, a line of gleaming coaches and carriages discharged their passengers and waited in a queue that stretched around the block and late into the night. W.C. was a gambling man, as everybody who read the papers knew, but he won more than he lost, and his brougham could be seen many nights standing in line on 44th Street.

Across the street from Delmonico's stood Sherry's, the ultimate dining experience. W.C. would dine in the lattice-vaulted palm room, then dance till dawn in the splendor of the Louis XVI ballroom. It was at Sherry's, in 1903, that C. K. G. Billings, the Chicago utility heir, gave a dinner for thirty-six guests, each mounted on a horse, each horse fitted with a table and hung with a champagne bucket. That same year, W.C. celebrated his sixty-second and last birthday at Sherry's. If he wanted fine food, Whitney went down the street to the Waldorf Astoria Hotel to see his friend Oscar Tschirky — Oscar of the Waldorf — but when he wanted pure ostentation, consumption on an epic scale, he came to the pleasure dome of Louis Sherry.

How did William Collins Whitney make his money?

The old-fashioned way: He married it.

Whitney — who had everything as a young man, according to one biographer, including "manly beauty, financial skill, business acumen, political shrewdness, magnetic talk, social grace, and irresistible charm" — lacked only money. The son of a merchant father of considerable but hardly princely means, Whitney had the good luck (or good sense) to befriend a fellow student at Yale named Oliver Payne. Payne's father had been an early partner of John D. Rockefeller, and Oliver went on to become part owner and treasurer of Rockefeller's Standard Oil empire. By all accounts an insufferable ass, Oliver had few friends and fewer scruples, but he did have a sister, Flora, a thoughtful if plain girl, who was just about the richest young debutante in the country. It seemed like the perfect match.

Access to the Payne family money allowed Whitney, upon graduating from Harvard Law School (one hundred years before Steve and me) to eschew more lucrative pursuits — temporarily at least — and put out his shingle in New York City as a reformer, determined to clean up the mess of graft and corruption left by the notorious Tweed Ring and its political stooges in Tammany Hall. As corporation counsel to the city, Whitney was able to curb many of the most extravagant abuses of the public trust and the public purse, abuses that had turned the awarding of government contracts into a massive patronage grabfest that cost the taxpayers of New York millions of unnecessary dollars.

But guarding the public treasury didn't pay nearly well enough to satisfy W.C.'s in-laws, not to mention his wife, Flora, who railed at him every night for spending *her* family's money instead of making some of his own. Eventually, Whitney realized that the only way to become a real robber baron (or at least a happy one) in the heyday of robber barons was not to marry money but to rob it. And so, in a complete reversal, Whitney the crusading "reformer," the Wasp Prince of Wall Street, turned everything he had learned about rooting out graft and corruption into a grand plan for making himself rich. So successful were his efforts that he soon earned himself a new nickname: The Grandee of Graft.

When Whitney found himself "outbid" on a city contract to build new trolley-car lines (another ambitious crook had offered bigger payoffs to the city aldermen), he leaked news of his competitor's bribes to the press and, capitalizing on his reputation as a reformer, stirred up a storm of protest that eventually scuttled the competing deal (worth $600,000) and landed his competitor (and a few aldermen) in jail. Whitney then moved in and bought the construction contract from his jailed competitor for a mere $25,000 — about four cents on the dollar.

But that was just the beginning. He then turned around and sold stock in the new venture for several times the original $600,000 value of the contract (and many, many times the price he paid for it). This practice, known as watering stock, was more or less legal in the Gilded Age of robber barons, before the Great Depression, before the Securities and Exchange Commission, even though it meant that lots of widows and orphans who bought watered stock often lost their life savings and piggy-bank change. Barons of social Darwinism like Whitney just considered that one of the risks of doing business in a truly free market.

And he wasn't done yet. Whitney took great pride in figuring out multiple ways to milk the same grand scam. To build a new trolley system, he would, of course, need lots of supplies — rails, streetcars, etc. — for which, under the terms of his contract, the city would reimburse him. Rather than buy his supplies on the open market, Whitney started up his own companies to produce them, companies that then submitted bills for dozens of times the actual costs of the goods supplied.

With an agreement by the city to reimburse his company for the purchase of any new rail lines added to the transit system, Whitney went out and found dozens of small lines, bought them in his own name at bargain prices, then sold them back to his company at dizzying markups — paying $250,000 for a trolley line one day, for example, then selling it the very next day for $965,000, pocketing $715,000 in profit. Or buying a money-losing horsecar line, with a third of a mile of tracks, ten aging cars, and thirty horses, for $15,000 one day, then selling $1 million worth of stock in it the next.

Whitney also brought a new level of Wall Street sophistication to the ancient Hibernian art of bribery. He would never be caught paying cash to city officials. Instead, he "reimbursed" them for favors, or paid them handsome lawyers' fees, or gave them profitable tips on the stock market, or offered them stock at ground-floor prices.

After only five years of wallowing in the mud he had once vowed to clean up, Whitney was rich: $40 million rich — at a time when $40 million really meant something. "His crimes," wrote one admiring chronicler of the excesses of the era, "were of such boldness and magnitude that even his cynical class was moved to astonishment." Of course, within another five years, the whole teetering edifice came crashing down, but by then Whitney had sold off all of his own stock in the company and, with the help of his blue-blooded, Harvard Law School–educated lawyer friends, successfully insulated himself from the legal consequences of the collapse. All those orphans and widows went to bed hungry, but no matter, W. C. Whitney was now a very rich man indeed.

Needless to say, money and social prominence weren't enough for W.C. He had to have power, too. So he went into politics — not on the stump, but behind the scenes. A

combination of Donald Trump and James Baker, or Ivan
Boesky and Lee Atwater. Tycoon and kingmaker. That was
W. C. Whitney.

Thanks to his personal charisma, aristocratic pedigree,
political experience, and business success, he quickly became the most powerful man in the Democratic Party —
the *only* man who could talk to all factions of the party during an especially fractious time in its history, organizing
them into a successful campaign to put a Democrat in the
White House, not once but twice — a remarkable feat
under any circumstances, but downright miraculous given
that the Democrat in question was Grover Cleveland, a cor-
pulent, alcoholic bachelor with little experience and even
less charisma. And Whitney made him *president*.

At a time when the president had the country in his
pocket, Whitney had the president in *his* pocket. Offered
his pick of jobs in Cleveland's cabinet, Whitney chose Secretary of the Navy and in just a few years completely over-
hauled a service that was still fighting the War of 1812. He
did everything, from converting the entire fleet to steel-
hulled ships (adding 93,951 tons in less than four years, almost all of it business for his friend Andrew Carnegie) to
redesigning officers' uniforms — bringing a "new smart-
ness" to the ranks. His efforts gave America the sea power
that helped make it, for the first time, a truly international
power and earned Whitney yet another sobriquet: Father of
the Modern Navy.

So successful was he in Washington, so powerful in the
Democratic Party, so ubiquitous in the press, and so rich,
that by the spring of 1896, everyone was talking "Whitney

for President." But W.C. wouldn't hear of it. He had something more important to do than be president: spend money.

As soon as he retired from politics, W. C. Whitney went on the most spectacular spending spree in American history. In the last twelve years of his life, Whitney spent $28 million — the equivalent of $500 million today. More than $40 million a year, $3 million a month, $100,000 *every single day* — including weekends and holidays — *for twelve years.*

And unlike fellow barons Rockefeller and Carnegie, Whitney didn't waste any of his money on the poor — on hospitals or schools or any other such charitable nonsense. W.C. gave not a thought to the plight of the poor or the sick or the stupid. He was strictly a social Darwinist. His charity was the Metropolitan Opera, and his idea of philanthropy was to rebuild the racetrack at Saratoga.

So where did all that money go? How did Whitney spend $28 million, or $500 million, or whatever, in so short a time?

The same way Steve and I would have.

On houses.

W. C. Whitney loved houses. Never in history — never in this country's history, anyway — has a man with the means to indulge that love, loved houses so much. He collected houses the way Lucky Dale collected, well, everything. His first, on the corner of Fifth Avenue and 57th Street, was given to him by his wife's family. Four stories of Romanesque brick and stone, capped by towers and soaring gables, it filled four city lots. But that was just the beginning.

Soon, he bought a five-thousand-acre country estate in Old Westbury, Long Island, and hired Stanford White to design a mammoth home and quarter-mile-long stables with stalls more luxurious than the servants' quarters. He bought seventy thousand acres in the Adirondacks, including fifty-two lakes, and built a baronial lodge, a golf course, and a railroad. He bought eleven thousand acres near Lenox, Massachusetts, stocked it with wild game, and built a rambling shingled cottage. He bought three thousand acres in Kentucky for a stud farm. He bought a one-hundred-fifty-year-old mansion with training stables and a private race-track in Brooklyn, right next to Coney Island. Then he bought another farm in Stony Ford, New York.

Eventually, he abandoned the huge house on 57th Street and built another, even grander one farther up Fifth Avenue, at 68th Street, a magnificent château filled with paintings by Tintoretto, Van Dyck, Millet, Reynolds, Cranach, and Filippo Lippi, and tapestries by Gobelin. It was said he had the tastes of a Medici. He and Stanford White went on buying trips and brought back not just furniture and art, but mantels, staircases, whole *rooms* plundered from the palaces of Europe.

In all, he collected nine city mansions and country estates, not counting the magnificent homes he rented in Maine and Kentucky, or the mansion in Washington, D.C., with a ballroom so big, it was said, you could turn a wagon around in it. Others, like his neighbors the Vanderbilts, may have had more money, some even had bigger houses, but no one, not Carnegie, not Mellon, not Rockefeller, not Morgan, *no one* had as many acres and homes as W.C. He owned more land in the states of New York and Massachusetts than anyone except the states themselves.

Henry Adams said of W.C., "After having gratified every

ambition, satiated every taste, gorged every appetite, won every object that New York afforded, and not yet satisfied, Whitney carried his field of activity abroad, until New York no longer knew what most to envy, his horses or his houses."

But envy they did. W. C. Whitney was the talk of New York. Almost every day, articles about him appeared in the city's newspapers. Every day, the public was treated to detailed stories about his parties, his family, his feuds, his vacations, his horses, and, of course, his houses. After all, in an era without movies or television or MTV or professional sports, there were only a few ways to achieve celebrity: as a socialite, a politician, a Croesus, or a crook. William Whitney was all of them.

Like celebrities in every era, of course, rock stars or royalty, Whitney was dogged by scandal. There were the usual whispered rumors of late-night visits to showgirls. And a certain amount of clucking and tsk-tsking among Fifth Avenue dowagers when he was seen in the Bohemian circle of Elsie De Wolfe, legendary interior decorator and leading lesbian of the city's homosexual elite.

But the real scandal didn't begin until Whitney's wife, Flora Payne, died suddenly in 1893, and W.C., after waiting the required three-year mourning period, married Mrs. Arthur Randolph, the widow of an English cavalry officer. Edith Sybil May Randolph was both a considerable wit and a great beauty, "with a perfect figure and wonderful coloring," according to the inevitable newspaper accounts. But she was also one of Flora Payne's best friends.

Flora's family was apoplectic. After years of watching Whitney use the Payne wealth to amass his own fortune, even as he cheated on Flora with every showgirl on Broadway, they considered his remarriage an act of ingratitude and betrayal. It didn't help that there had been rumors about a liaison between W.C. and Edith Randolph even before Flora's death. Brother-in-law Oliver Payne was especially indignant. A lifelong bachelor who had practically moved in with the Whitneys during Flora's lifetime (he had an apartment in their Fifth Avenue mansion), Oliver broke off all contact with W.C. and vowed publicly to destroy him on Wall Street. "Oliver Payne has sworn solemnly to take William C. Whitney's wealth away from him," a prominent lawyer reported at the time. "Payne ... swore that he would take every cent away from Whitney that he secured by reason of his former marriage."

In a bald effort to destroy Whitney's family as well as his fortune, Oliver approached each of W.C.'s four children with a stunning offer: If they renounced their father, Oliver would make them heirs to his considerably greater fortune. And given the way Whitney Sr. was spending money, he pointedly reminded them, there wouldn't be much left when Daddy died. Only two of Whitney's children stuck by their father. Two agreed to Uncle Oliver's Faustian bargain, and one of them, W.C.'s second son, William Payne, even agreed to drop his first name — his father's name — and refer to himself thereafter simply as Payne Whitney.

To escape the familial wars, the rumors, and the scandal sheets, Whitney did what he always did: bought another house. This time, he bought a little country inn in a small southern town where he had stayed while visiting friends. It also happened to be the town where he had first rendezvoused with Edith Randolph. In some ways, this house, his tenth, was for her. The town was a center of horse activity, and Edith loved horses as well as horsemen.

The town was Aiken.

And, after Whitney completed a series of elaborate additions, the little country inn, purchased from a Charleston woman named Sarah Joye, was transformed into Joye Cottage.

13.

Slippery Conditions on the Information Highway

Within just a few days of Steve's encounter with Frank Hatch, the rumor that Madonna was coming to Aiken had spread (fanned, no doubt, by Frank) to every corner of town and every conversation at the drugstore, bank, or dry cleaner's. As a rule, the younger the gossips, the more likely they were to welcome the startling news. The thirtysomething pharmacist thought it would be great for the town because "it would bring lots of other Hollywood people here." A twentysomething clerk at Blockbuster Video summed up her feelings in one word: "Cool."

But older residents weren't so sure. Did this woman with

one name have anything to contribute to their town? "I don't know," said one white-haired doyenne as she picked up a half-dozen floral print dresses at the dry cleaner's. "I don't think she would really fit into Aiken society." (The mind boggled at the image of Madonna dressing up in a floral print dress, pearls, and hat for the Tuesday luncheon at the Bellwether Club — Aiken's most exclusive, geriatric, and soporific social venue — for a lively afternoon of bridge and golf talk.) "Of course," our white-haired doyenne added ominously, "I doubt that her application to the club would be approved." Express *that*, you shameless hussy.

Within a week, rumor was rampant on a field of ignorance. First we heard that Madonna had looked at the Knox house, called The Balcony, a gracious brick house on twelve acres with the best stables in town. It was built by Seymour Knox, a fabulously wealthy banker in the tradition of J. P. Morgan and one of the founders of the Albright-Knox Art Museum in Buffalo, who had wintered in Aiken for sixty years before his recent death.

Then we heard that she liked Ridgelea Hall, a big, formidable manse that had once been converted into a nunnery. The Catholic Church had closed it down, shipped off the nuns, and put the old house up for sale, but a wrought-iron cross still capped the roof, raising all sorts of sacrilegious possibilities that might intrigue a wayward Catholic girl. Papa Don't Preach. Then we heard she wanted the Pink House, a sprawling Bel Air–style hacienda with beautiful stables just across Easy Street from Joye Cottage.

Then we heard she wanted *Joye Cottage*. That, at least, was a rumor we could squelch with total assurance.

The frenzy of gossip lasted for weeks. There were even

reported sightings of the elusive blond star — placing her variously at the Quik-shop, the Shell station, and Bobby's Bar-B-Q. (Like Elvis, she apparently had a taste for colorful, unlikely venues.) So when it came my turn to visit Frank for a haircut, I was looking forward to an update on the *real* story.

"What's the latest on Madonna?" I asked even before sitting down.

Frank laughed. "Oh, she never came to Aiken."

"What do you mean?" I was crushed. Truth be told, Steve and I had already made plans to offer her our Rolodex of workers and give her a tour of the project. Just being neighborly, of course.

"It was all a big rumor," said Frank.

"How do you know?" I demanded.

"Because *I* started it," said Frank with another big laugh.

"But why?"

Frank shrugged his shoulders as he came at me with scissors and comb. "I don't know. I got bored."

14.

Illusions of Grandeur

William Whitney, Madonna, Steve, and I were not the only ones with visions of living in a palace.

One day, Jeff "It wasn't me" Watson didn't come back from his lunch break. An hour later, the police called to tell us he was under arrest. He had been seen walking into Kroger's grocery store (pronounced Krogé by locals mocking such big-city pretensions as a health-food aisle) wearing a long winter coat. A few minutes later, he walked out, without stopping at the cashier, wearing two sixteen-ounce T-bone steaks. Alerted by the sight of a man in a winter coat in ninety-degree weather, store security followed his juice trail to the parking lot, where they arrested him.

Now he wanted us to bail him out.

After letting him stew overnight, we paid his bail and picked him up. While incarcerated, the deputy on duty told us, Jeff had passed the time by painting a mural on the wall of his cell with food coloring from the jail kitchen. The deputy, a youngish man with an oldish, Elmer Fudd face, had seen the articles about us and the house in the paper and was eager to show us this unusual cell-block Sistine. "You jest won't b'leeve it," he kept saying as he led us back to the holding area.

He was right. There on the cinderblock walls was the image of a big white house. It was Joye Cottage, all right — no mistake about it — with the addition of six small, crudely drawn figures arranged around a car in front. It looked like an ad for a luxury automobile done in finger paint. When asked to explain, Jeff said proudly: "That's mah house."

And the car?

"That's mah Roils Royce."

And the figures around it?

Jeff smiled. "That's three prostitutes, two pimps, and a poodle."

15.

Cherchez le Barbecue

When not viewed from the moral high ground, Jeff's pur-
loined tenderloin could be seen as just another example of
the never-ending search for a good meal. Not long after we
moved to Aiken and just as work on the house was about to
begin, a friend sent us a copy of Peter Mayle's book *A Year
in Provence.* Informed that it was about a writer who moved
to southern France and renovated an old farmhouse, we
tore into it hungrily. Surely there would be some helpful advice and some consoling laughs for two American writers
who had moved to the American South (a far more exotic
land) to renovate an old house.

But to our astonishment, and disappointment, that wasn't what the book was about at all. Mayle was only intermittently interested in houses. His chief love, the real subject of his book, was *food*. On every page, it seemed, there were rapturous, lyrical accounts of five-star-worthy meals, of lamb stuffed with herbs and veal stuffed with truffles, all prepared by colorful, crinkly eighty-year-old chefs with vinaigrette for blood, in charming little restaurants in converted old mills on out-of-the-way country lanes, or something, far from the madding crowd of German tourists. A "simple" meal at a restaurant in Buoux, for example — a town too small to be called a village — would begin with fourteen different exotic hors d'oeuvres, followed by lamb cooked in whole cloves of garlic, baby green beans, and a potato-and-onion *galette*, topped off by a cheese from Banon and a troika of desserts — lemon sorbet, chocolate tart, and *crème Anglaise*. Or how about a peasant feast of rabbit, boar, and thrush pâtés, duck smothered in gravy and heaped with wild mushrooms, or a steaming rabbit casserole, topped off with an almond and cream gâteau, and on and on.

And what was the second-most-important subject in Mayle's book? Was it plumbing or lighting or dry rot or the advantages of fixed contracts over hourly rates — all things that would have been of urgent interest to us? Not at all. It was *booze*. Actually, *booze* is far too crude a term for the rivers of wine, beer, liqueur, and everything else invented by man to quench a hearty Provençal thirst that flowed through the pages of Mayle's book: a brilliant red Côtes du Rhône from Visan; a Châteauneuf-du-Pape that spent the afternoon breathing in the shade; a locally produced *digestif* prepared from an eleventh-century recipe conceived by a group of monks in the Basses-Alpes; and on and on. The farmhouse apparently fixed itself while Mayle staggered from dusty green bottle to dusty green bottle making notes.

Not that it wasn't a wonderful book. But helpful? Not. It did suggest, however, that if we were really interested in *experiencing* our new *pays*, we would have to go out and search for the food that truly defined it, the quintessential food that conveyed all the color and flavor and charm and simple down-home country goodness of a Carolina dawn.

▲

From the moment we sat down at the soiled gingham oil-cloth at Georgialina Bar-B-Q, we knew we were in for something, well . . . special. Friends had cautioned us with a smile, "It's nothing fancy, but the barbecue is the best in town."

More like out of town. The car ride was nearly twenty minutes, which, in a bizarre way, seemed very promising. We remembered all those out-of-the-way cafés and back-road inns that Mayle had discovered while roaming the countryside between fits of renovation. Surely, if people were willing to travel so far from home, the fare must be truly exceptional. We had also been told that the place was family-owned — another good sign — and was open only three nights a week. But when we arrived and asked to meet the owner, we were told that he had taken his RV to Myrtle Beach — as he did, apparently, whenever the restaurant was open during the summer.

The decor was, well . . . basic. Cinderblock walls, painted gray, as close as we could tell. The tables were picnic tables, a charming, rustic touch, covered with the aforementioned gingham oilcloths, which were neither charming nor rustic, just dirty. Fluted plastic salt-and-pepper shakers completed the table settings.

The service was, well . . . basic. In fact, there wasn't any. It didn't take us long to realize that if we continued to sit, we would never eat at all. There were two lines, snaking along either side of the large room toward a cafeteria buffet like the one in grade school — fiberglass trays, paper plates, plastic utensils, a long horizontal metal grill, and, behind it, tray after tray of steaming food.

It was an evening of many surprises. The first was the meat. When I think of barbecue, I think of spare ribs or chicken or hunks of beef braised in some tart, secret-formula sauce and broiled over an open flame. That, we discovered, was some damn city-bred Yankee notion of barbecue. *Real* barbecue, southern barbecue, didn't look like meat at all, but more like a pale brown gruel, a kind of lumpy oatmeal mixed with gravy. There was meat there, all right, in strands as thin as floss and strange gristly nodules that made me want to forget everything I knew about porcine anatomy.

I asked the lady in front of me, who looked fit enough to be an aerobics instructor and therefore reasonably reliable, what was in the barbecue. "Hash," she chirped. And in the hash? "You don't want to know."

Then, after a pause, she offered in partial explanation: "I wandered out back once, where a big man was carving some meat off a carcass, but when he saw me he pointed a huge knife in my direction and chased me away."

The rest of the meal was pretty much to match. The corn was decobbed (by the Jolly Green Giant, not by the absent owner-operator). There were buckets of fried grits, fried fritters, and fried chicken wings. "You can come back for more as often as you like," the man behind me in line offered helpfully. I could see by the fold of flesh that hung out between his T-shirt and his belt that he had done exactly that.

We decided not to embarrass ourselves by asking about wine. The only drinks in sight were the two plastic pitchers of iced tea, Magic Markered "sweet" and "unsweet," sitting next to the cash register for convenient help-yourself service. In place of crusty, golden brown baguettes were loaves of white sandwich bread, still in their cellophane wrappers.

Back at the soiled gingham oilcloth, we dug in. And, truth be told, it wasn't bad. That much fried cholesterol rests pretty happily on the tongue if not on the conscience, the hips, or the heart. The cost of our first genuine Carolina repast: $7.75 for a complete meal for two. Eat your heart out, Peter Mayle.

16.

This Old Palace

Back at the house, we had work to do. And now, thanks to a very generous contract to write two true-crime books, we had the money to do it.

How much work? When Steve and I toured the house with a yellow legal pad making a *preliminary* list of things to do, it ran to forty pages. By lunchtime.

Take the bathroom.

Please.

Most of the water lines in the house were made of galvanized iron with lead joints. All would have to be replaced, even those cemented inside the walls and floors. The old cast-iron waste pipes were clogged and leaked at every joint. All would have to be replaced. The hardware on the sink and tub — the faucets, the drains, the spouts, the plugs — all missing. Replacements? For hundred-year-old fixtures? Would new ones fit? The toilet wasn't a toilet at all, but a water closet — seat below, box above, long chain between — and hadn't worked in, what, twenty years? Thirty? Fifty? Try getting spare parts for that. And where would we put a shower?

The big marble vanity was missing its sink (a unique size, no doubt) and had cracked in two like a great big bar of white chocolate. It would need repair. How do you repair hundred-year-old, two-inch-thick Carrara marble? Elmer's Glue? The mahogany doors, beautiful once, were blistered and bleached and wouldn't open — too many unheated winters and uncooled summers. We looked in the basement and found a dirty, rough spot on the floor where the boiler used to be. There was even a pile of leftover coal nearby.

Every surface in the room had suffered from the same inexorable push-pull of temperature extremes: grout separating from tile, wood from wall, paint from plaster, plaster from lath, lath from studs. On the ceiling, the plaster was breaking up like ice on a pond. In the windows, not just the glass was broken, but the sashes, too. And all the wiring would have to be replaced. Too dangerous. The old light fixtures, black with tarnish, hung by their frayed innards.

And that was just one of *sixteen* bathrooms — one of the best ones, in fact. And then there were the other forty-four rooms, some in better shape, some in considerably worse.

What experience did we have? Surely, two people who set out to rescue a sixty-room house from the jaws of the wrecking crane and bring it back to glorious life on a less-than-glorious budget must be wizards of the building trades, masters of everything from metalwork to marbleizing, do-it-yourselfers *par excellence*. Surely, only someone with vast, encyclopedic experience in building and renovation would undertake such a project.

Well, it depends on what you mean by experience. Experience in designing five-hundred-room palaces? Sure. Experience in fantasizing construction on an imperial scale? Loads. Experience actually *building?* Well, I did watch my father build a one-room plywood clubhouse in our backyard once (which I soon saw deconstructed with chilling ease by the neighborhood bully). Then, when I was eight, Artie Cosler and I built a treehouse — although it was barely big enough to hold the two of us and it didn't have any walls.

I guess my first *real* experience with construction was following my father around as he supervised the building of a string of Howard Johnson's motels and restaurants across the Midwest. (Motels, not construction, was his business, but he, too, was a do-it-yourselfer.) My brother and I played war in the foundation trenches, fingered our initials in slabs of new-laid concrete, clambered over framing beams to lob crab apples at the workers, and generally made nuisances of ourselves.

By age seven or eight, I knew what plumbers did, and what carpenters did, and what neither of them would do (Columbus, Ohio, being a union town). I knew that electricians were usually the smartest people on a job site, plumbers, the nicest. But I never listened to my father and the workmen for long, especially after they stopped cursing and joking and started thrashing out the details of circuit loads and circulating pumps, or the esoterica of air conditioning and drywall finishing. I had wars to fight.

So, with nothing more than foggy childhood memories and a dozen episodes of *This Old House* under our belts, Steve and I set out to resurrect Mr. Whitney's winter palace.

Crazy? Absolutely. But not stupid. We knew we needed help — help in knowing what needed to be done; help in knowing when to do what; help in knowing who to hire to do it; help in knowing what to ask them, what to expect, what to pay; help even in knowing what we needed help in knowing. We called Wilma, our real estate agent, and told her our problem. She responded without hesitation, "Bubba."

Excuse me?

"Bubba. Bubba Barnes."

Now, even as someone with a cousin named Bub I have a hard time putting my trust in any adult who answers to the name Bubba. So it was with considerable trepidation that I watched the old black pickup bearing the plastic laminate sign "Barnes Construction" pull into the driveway of Joye Cottage. The man who unfolded from behind the wheel was a tall, lanky fellow, slightly stooped, with jowls like old saddlebags mottled with age. Judging from his metallic gray hair and the white in his stubble, he had to be in his fifties at least. He wore an old Clemson baseball cap that, from the frayed, faded look of it, might have been his own in undergraduate days. Or maybe not.

One thing for sure, he was no Bob Vila.

"Looks like y'all bit off a mouthful," he said with a big, toothy grin.

After shaking our hands in his viselike, sandpaper grip, he listened with his head cocked as we explained what we needed from him. Because we couldn't afford to pay a contractor the standard 20 percent fee, we would be hiring and supervising the workmen ourselves. To do that, we needed to know, well, just about everything.

The completeness of our ignorance didn't faze him a bit. "Why don't we look see what we got," he said, taking in the whole house with a long, skeptical squint.

I figured he would want to see the outside first, take a walk around, look the place over. But no. "Let's start in the basement," he said with a strange, crooked half smile. "Basements don't lie."

At this point it would be helpful to provide some geography.

Joye Cottage takes roughly — very roughly — the form of an H. Think of an H with two broken legs. Or a bow-legged H. That's Joye Cottage. The lower right leg is the kitchen and dining wing; the lower left leg is the guest wing, with five bedrooms and bathrooms; the upper right "arm" is the ballroom wing; the upper left arm is the master bedroom wing; and the crossbar — by far the biggest section of the H — is everything else: foyer, salon, library, billiard room, sitting room, etc. All five parts of the H (the four wings and the center section) have second floors filled with bedrooms.

We followed Bubba into the basement, a part of the house we had toured only once before, on our first visit. At that time, none of the lights worked, and the cloudy win-

dows obscured the occasional ray of sunlight. Every time I tried to say something — register fear or disgust mostly — a film of cobwebs would float out of the darkness and into my mouth. It had rained for several days before our arrival, and the floor was inches deep in black, oily water. We could tell from the rotten old walk boards that this was not an uncommon state; that, among basements, ours was the equivalent of a tidal marsh, a permanently semiaquatic environment — a fact that was dramatically confirmed when the beam of our flashlight startled a little knot of water snakes into squirmy flight.

With that memory vividly in mind, we followed Bubba down into the darkness at the bottom of the stairs.

This time, thankfully, there was no water on the floor, although Bubba took pains to point out the dry, mummified remains of a frog as we passed, commenting sagely, "Where there's frogs, there's water."

Bubba's basement tour turned up some interesting surprises. The kitchen wing, the lower right leg of the H, was the oldest part of the house, the remnant of its beginnings as a farmhouse, as old as anything Bubba had seen in the area, probably 1830s. He could tell because the bricks in the foundation were handmade from clay on the site. He took time to admire the big beams that held up the floor above, a foot thick, a foot deep, and brown as molasses. "That's hewn, not sawn," he pointed out. "There's a lot of back in those timbers." He took his knife and stabbed one of them hard. The blade barely stuck. "Heart pine. Hard as rock."

He found a spot where the wood had splintered and pried off a piece with his knife. "Smell that," he said, offering up the splinter like a wafer. The heavy basement air filled with the sweet musk of pine sap. "Loblolly pine. Been here a hundred years and it still smells like the day it was cut. There's no wood better for building a house." He held the splinter up to the light to show how the sap still glistened.

According to Bubba the archaeologist, the dining room — a big room that connected the kitchen wing to the main house — had been added "after the war" (the Civil War, we presumed). The boards and bricks were imported and most of the timbers machine milled, probably at one of the big sawmills in Augusta. "Aiken had its first big buildin' boom in the eighteen seventies," said Bubba the historian, "when it became a popular winter resort and a lot of folks expanded their houses to take in boarders."

Bubba also discovered that the billiard room, the next

room in line after the dining room, had once been a barn or shed or some kind of outbuilding, but when they built the dining room, they connected the shed to the old farmhouse and enclosed it, adding yet another room to what was becoming, in the words of Bubba the architecture critic, "a ramblin' mess."

But the worst news was yet to come. While inspecting the brick foundation walls under the main wing (the crossbar of the H), Bubba exclaimed, "I knew it!" as he snatched the Clemson cap from his head and flung it to the ground in disgust. "This whole dang place was designed by an *architect!*"

Not just an architect, but a "*Yankee* architect."

When we expressed surprise that this should distress him so, Bubba launched into an impassioned attack on the integrity, intelligence, parentage, and manhood of architects. "See them walls?" he fumed, pointing his flashlight at what looked to us like a plain brick foundation wall. "Those go down another three feet at least. That's a foundation for ground that freezes — hard. That's a — a —" he searched for a sufficiently disparaging term, "a *Connecticut* foundation. That's what you get when you let an architect design a house."

He ranted on. "They put in doors and windows wherever they please. Don't matter whether they fall natural or not. You leave a carpenter to do his work, and he'll put the windows and doors where they belong — between the studs. Saves cuts, saves wood, saves time, saves work, saves money. But no! When an architect says he wants a window here, then a window's gotta go *here.* So you gotta add more studs, cut some scabs. Dang. You can't tell me it would make any difference if that window was six inches this way or six inches that way. Six inches and it cost 'em half a day. That's an architect for you."

Bubba's final, and most amazing, discovery was that the main part of the house, the big 40-by-100-foot crossbar of the H that W. C. Whitney added when he bought the place in 1896, had been built at one time and, according to Bubba, was completed, start to finish, *in six weeks* — "eight weeks tops!" Now, I didn't know a lot about construction, I admit, but I did know that in New York it had taken six weeks to get a set of bookshelves built.

How could Bubba tell?

He gave us the same crooked smile that said "stupid city boys," then showed us where two big floor joists had been laid within just inches of each other. "Normally, they lay these big joists starting at one side and going to the other," he explained expansively. "But here they were in such a hurry that they had gangs layin' 'em from both sides simultaneously, workin' towards the middle."

All this sounded to Steve and me a little like tea-leaf reading or seeing auguries in the entrails of chickens. Bubba sensed our skepticism. "It don't matter how many people they had driving nails," he conceded, "there's only one way they could have finished this job in six weeks." With that, he led us out of the basement, up the salon stairs, through a scuttle hole in the ceiling of a second-floor closet, and in among the roof rafters. Darkness to darkness. The result was climatic whiplash, from the cool, damp basement to the hot, dry attic.

We weren't there but a few seconds before Bubba let out a little whoop of triumph, *"Aaeeeeeeuuuuuuuup! I knew it!"* and threw down his cap again. Shining his light on the under-side of a rafter, he showed us a big black stain on an other-wise golden timber, then another stain on another timber, then another. "Those spots come from oil lamps," he ex-plained. "They got the frame up and then finished the job *by lamplight*. Dang, they were in a hurry!" He reached up for his cap, but finding it already used for punctuation, scratched his metallic hair instead.

Suddenly, sitting in the roof rafters, I had a vision of a hundred workmen crawling over the skeleton of Joye Cot-tage from dawn till dusk and past, sawing and hacking at beams the size of ships' keels, toting bundles of heart-pine flooring and great armfuls of lath for the plasterers, all by the yellow light of oil lamps while above, in the very place where we sat balanced precariously in the hot, dusty darkness, carpenters hived among the rafters in the starry night air.

17.

Immortality

After our encounter with Bubba Barnes, we revised all our lists, collected and totaled all the estimates, negotiated and signed all the contracts (heating, air conditioning, plumbing, electrical, etc.), and then, finally, after all the talking and signing, the moment came when we were ready to *start*. Ready to *do* something.

But what? The laborers had pretty much finished the cleanup and cleanout. Until the workmen actually arrived, what could *we* do? There the house stood, in all its ramshackle glory, waiting for us to begin. But where? With twenty thousand square feet and every square foot in need of urgent attention, where do you start?

Armed with my gray plastic toolbox from Ace, I walked up to the front door — a massive thing — and started unscrewing.

Ever since childhood, I've had a thing about brass. When I was in seventh grade, we moved into a new house, and I was in charge of polishing all the hardware — doorknobs, faceplates, keyhole covers, hinges, window pulls, the works. I spent weeks with my hands immersed in some milky, sulfurous solution that turned a vile, bilious green on contact with tarnish. But when I was finished — God, what a spectacle. That old, black, paint-covered junk had turned the most brilliant, glorious gold. A pile of scrap metal had been transformed into Montezuma's ransom. The alchemy of it dazzled me.

Looking back, I suppose that was the first time I experienced the joy of renovation — the joy of taking something old and making it new again. The first time I felt like I'd struck a blow against impermanence; a blow against time; a blow against mortality. Years later, when I watched the pictures sent back by those deep-diving cameras from the wrecks of the *Titanic* and the *Bismarck,* and saw brass fittings lying on the ocean floor, miles down, I thought, "Damn, those should shine up just great." Didn't matter how long they'd been down there, how black they'd gotten, brass could always come back. With enough rubbing and enough vile bilious-green solution, time could be turned backward in its flight.

There was a time when almost every house built in America was fitted out with brass. Not just the Joye Cottages, either, but little houses like the ones down by the woods, where the stable hands stayed — solid-brass doorknobs with solid-brass plates held in place by solid-brass screws. A huge industry developed to keep America supplied with cheap, solid, eternal brass. Everybody had at least a few pieces of immortality. Now, of course, even "nice" houses, tract mansions and the like, use plated brass, or worse. In a few years, the brassness wears off, molecule by molecule, each time someone opens a door. The brass industry in America is virtually gone — a thin vestigial plate of its former self, catering to eccentric purists and crackpot preservationists. Hardware, like housing, has become disposable.

By the time I finished unscrewing, I had collected as many as 28 individual pieces of brass (not including screws) from *each* of 146 windows and 128 doors.

This much immortality could kill us.

18.

Bedford Falls Syndrome

Speaking of mortality, of all the irritating aspects of life in New York, none was more likely to make one contemplate the evanescence of life than standing in line at the post office.

Where do postal employees in New York learn their Chinese-water-torture approach to service? Do they take seminars in how to walk more and more slowly as the line grows longer and longer, eventually achieving an Einsteinian state of arrested motion at the precise moment the line curls out the door and into the cold, drizzly street? Standing in line on Columbus Avenue once, I remember thinking that it isn't really surprising that postal workers so often go on murderous tears, killing fellow workers and themselves in explosions of frustration and rage; what's surprising is that postal *customers* so rarely do likewise.

So you can imagine our amazement when we walked into the Aiken post office for the first time and saw *no lines!* Just two smiling ladies, Mary and Terry, dressed in immaculate uniforms and standing behind an immaculate counter.

Mary and Terry exhibited the extraordinary diplomatic adroitness to look at the names on our packages as well as the mental acuity to *remember* them. It's hard to believe, but after only a few trips, they not only smiled at us but welcomed us *by name*. After a few more trips, they began to ask questions ("How is the work on the house going?" "Did those L. L. Bean boots fit?"). Before long, an acquaintanceship was born. Not a friendship, really — we didn't know their spouses, or kids, or even if they had any, and I could never keep their names straight (now, which one is Mary?) — but the conversation was pleasant enough to loosen the knot of anxiety that always used to accompany those little pink summonses to the post office on Columbus Avenue.

Mary and Terry weren't the only ones, either. Aiken's main drag, Laurens Street, was lined with quaint, friendly, pastel shops and salespeople to match: the lady at the shoe repair shop who baked cakes on the side (so the smells of leather and sugar were always competing); the pharmacist who called your name and waved from his aerie at the back of the store as soon as you walked in the door; the clothier who didn't mind if you took the merchandise home and tried it out *before* paying (and, no doubt, lamented our preference for sweatpants and shorts); the florist who knew everybody's taste in flowers ("Whatever you do, don't send her anything red. She *hates* red"). These and others turned every trip downtown into a mini-reunion — Mr. Rogers goes shopping — as distant from the gauntlet of Columbus Avenue as Woodstock was from Watts.

There was a danger lurking here, however; a new danger, one that we had never faced in New York and therefore didn't recognize at first. We came to call it "Bedford Falls Syndrome," after Jimmy Stewart's Christmas card of a hometown in *It's a Wonderful Life*. What harm could there be in idling for a few minutes of friendly conversation over a registered letter or postage-due package? And then moving on to the bank (where there were also *no lines*) for another neighborly exchange with Annie, the teller, who can't wait to tell us about a church-sponsored trip to the Country Music Hall of Fame? And then to the photo lab, where the owners' son — sweet, amiable Barney — wants to share his thoughts on Rush Limbaugh's latest show and invite us to the Church of God cookout the following Sunday ("Good people and good food," he advertises. "Can't beat that combination")?

Suddenly, three quick errands have turned into an entire afternoon of friendly, back-fence badinage — and more time has gone by than if I *had* been stuck in lines. Long lines. So much pleasantness can be scary. After a while, I start thinking about another old film depicting small-town life, *Invasion of the Body Snatchers*.

The worst case of BFS I ever encountered was on a trip to the hardware store downtown to have some keys copied. Now, admittedly, having keys copied for Joye Cottage wasn't like having the apartment key copied in New York. At the time — before we standardized the locks — the house had twenty-three exterior doors, which required twelve separate keys. We needed six copies of each key, or seventy-two keys altogether.

I should have known I was in trouble the moment I walked in. There was a line — only one person, but in Aiken, one person constitutes a line. The lady behind the key counter, a grandmotherly type with a chain on her glasses, smiled benevolently at me as I entered, but her attention never wandered from the man in front of me, who was in the middle of a description of his most recent flare-up of colitis, a description that rivaled, in detail, anything in Proust.

I could see by the way the woman fingered the two keys in her hand that she had long since completed her part of this transaction. But it was at least another five minutes before she handed the customer his keys, took his money, and made change, while nodding with considerable concern through a closing summary of his most recent visit to a gastroenterologist in Augusta.

When it was finally my turn, I handed her the twelve keys and told her I needed six copies of each. "How long do you think this will take?" I coaxed.

She gave me a smile that would have inspired Norman Rockwell. "Not long, sugar," she said in the sweet, honeyed voice of a sweet old southern woman who had spent her whole life practicing to be a sweet old southern woman someday.

That's when the torture began. Launching into a full history of her family — all fourteen grandchildren's worth —

she set to work. With the care and deliberateness of a Dead Sea Scroll scholar piecing together fragments of a new gospel, she took one of my original keys and compared it with what seemed like three hundred blanks, holding each one up to the light, one by one, squinting through her bifocals, looking for the perfect match — the precise size and configuration that would guarantee a perfect copy. Finally, after an especially thorough discussion of Buffie's fourth-grade report on the Gullahs (inhabitants of the sea islands off the South Carolina coast), she made her first match and a wave of humble satisfaction washed gently — and very slowly — over her.

That was one.

I, of course, complimented her lavishly on this success, in the Skinnerian hope that this might speed the process. But when I handed her Key Number Two, she waved it away. Before we could go on, she had to make six copies of Key Number One — and tell me all about Freddie, who had just been selected captain of his high school football team and applied for admission to Duke. She inserted the original into the metal grip of the machine beside her and turned on the motor. She inserted the first blank. She pressed the blank against the rotating blades of the machine, following the bumps and hollows of the original. Sparks flew and the raucous grinding noise filled the store, but neither sparks nor din could shake the benevolent smile from that powdery face. She ran the blade back and forth over the blank with the care of a Renaissance goldsmith fashioning a chalice for the pope, then burnished it to a jewellike perfection.

That was one.

Only seventy-one more to go.

As the afternoon light faded into dusk — and she ran through the entire gamut from Christie, age two, through Rodney, age nineteen, and I began to fear that her grandchildren would have children of their own before the task was completed — I ruminated further on the nature of neighborly banter, benign smiles from behind counters, and *Invasion of the Body Snatchers.* Politeness leads to neighborliness, leads to lost afternoons, leads to missed deadlines. Maybe New York had the right answer, after all. Maybe lines were safer.

I told her I had to go, that I would return the next day and pick up the keys. Then I offered to leave a deposit.

"Oh, no, sugar," she said in that same voice with that same smile. "I trust you."

Never mind about New York.

19.

The First Noel

(1897)

Back at Joye Cottage, the hunt for the Whitney Silver had one unforeseen benefit: It opened up to exploration regions of the house unseen by human eyes since the dawn of the auto age. Like those little motorized cameras that scan ancient shipwrecks miles down in the deep, the light from our laborers' flashlights scanned the darkest bowels of crawl-space and attic, areas that had last been lit by oil lamps.

On one such dive, the scanning light fell on the withered brown remains of a Christmas wreath, so brittle that it turned to ashes in my hand. But the satin bow was still in place, and its hand-stitched message still readable:

"Merry Christmas, W.C."

When W. C. Whitney opened Joye Cottage for the first time, in December 1897, he was one of the richest men in America. So when he threw a Christmas party, people came. Outside Joye Cottage's massive front door clad in freshly minted brass, a line of carriages garlanded with holly and liveried coachmen bore the grandest names of New York society: Vanderbilt and Sloane, Hitchcock and Burden. In their private train cars, accompanied by legions of servants, they came from New York City, Long Island, Chicago, and Europe to pay their respects and to see Mr. Whitney's fabulous new winter home. The *New York Times* sent a reporter and a photographer to whip up a soufflé spread for the paper's fledgling Sunday feature, the "Illustrated Magazine."

For six months, in fact, society pages in all the New York papers had been following the reconstruction of Joye Cottage; retelling the tale of how "Mr. W" had enjoyed his first visit to Aiken in 1896 so much that he returned there and bought a well-known boarding establishment, Sarah Joye's Inn; how, with the help of his good friend architect Stanford White, he planned additions that more than quadrupled the size of the old hostelry; and how he had surprised all his friends by hiring the young firm of Carrère & Hastings — recent winner of a design contest for the grand new public library on Fifth Avenue — to draw up the plans and oversee the work.

To finish the job in time for Mr. W's Christmas party, the local contractor had kept a crew of one hundred men at work from dawn till dusk and beyond. Huge trees from nearby stands of virgin pine were mule-hauled to the site and cut down to size with two-man saws and teams of axmen. The big ten-by-twenty-inch beams were laid on seventeen-inch-thick brick foundations, then slathered black with creosote to protect them from termites, and bundles of heart-pine flooring were brought in by train from nearby mills in Augusta. According to one newspaper account, the people of little Aiken were so astonished by this New York–sized and New York–paced construction project that they stopped their buggies on Easy Street and gawked for hours. The question on everyone's mind — especially the contractor's, no doubt: Would it be finished in time?

Fortunately, this society-page cliff-hanger had a happy ending. By the time W.C. and his new bride, Edith, arrived in Aiken by private train in December, the last coat of paint was dry, all sixty rooms had been hastily filled with furniture (most of it reproductions from Grand Rapids), every pillow on every couch was fringed, every fireplace filled with wood, and every new pane of glass cleaned to the squeak. Even the big Christmas tree in the salon was aloft and alight.

The house never looked better than it did that day, festooned with swags of pine rope laced with the orange-red berries of holly and the white of mistletoe, lit by sputtering fatwood fires and five hundred scented candles.

But like so many great houses', Joye Cottage's fate followed that of the ruling class. One by one, Whitney's descendants retreated from the suburban sprawl of rooms that the family patriarch had built. Lured by more glamorous watering holes, bled of their servants, and increasingly burdened by the expensive ritual of opening and closing a great house, especially for only a few weeks or months a year, successive generations of Whitneys surrendered the house, room by room, to the creeping leaks, the blistering heat, the maundering mildew, the bleaching sunshine, the prying tendrils of ivy and wisteria, and the indefatigable legions of carpenter ants. With so many rooms, it was easier to abandon than to fix.

By the time the last Whitney left the house, in 1980, only the ballroom wing remained in use. By the time we bought it, a decade later, the rest of the house had been abandoned for so long that neighbors began to see ghosts in the tricky windows and hear music drifting out from the long-empty rooms at night; abandoned for so long that local teenagers routinely held clandestine parties in the dark, distant wings, necking by moonlight in the tricky windows and dancing to their muted radios in the grand spaces once reserved for the barons of American commerce.

It wasn't much, but other than the pageant of insect survival that went on in every corner, it was the only sign of life left in the great hulking carcass of W.C.'s Christmas dream.

One day a policeman dropped by the work site. Not the Deputy Dawg we had encountered after Jeff Watson's night in the county jail, but a trim young man in blue, with razor creases in his pants and a clipped blond moustache. He introduced himself simply as Paul and explained that he had been the caretaker of Joye Cottage during the infamous Mr. Kane's reign of error. He just wanted to check out the progress of the renovation.

As Steve and I showed him around, he regaled us with

stories of Kane's neglect, and his frustration. Kane wouldn't authorize any money for repairing the skylights, or the gutters, or the flashing, or anything else, he said. Only when Sotheby's came to take pictures for the brochure did he shell out anything, and then only enough for paint — cheap paint — and only for the facades and rooms that would be photographed. It was nothing less than a miracle, he said, that the place was still standing.

How much of a miracle came as a surprise even to us. "You know that Kane had given me the order to start demolishing the house," Officer Paul told us. "He had a salvage company come in to appraise all the fixtures so he'd know what to take out before knocking it down."

We had always fancied that we snatched Joye Cottage from the path of the wrecking ball. Now, it turned out, we actually did.

20.

Just Glenn

One morning not long after the crew of laborers had begun their work of deconstruction, Steve and I arrived early from our temporary quarters in the squash court to discover that somebody had been using a window seat in the salon as a bed. Whoever it was had borrowed several packing blankets from our New York furniture (which would remain mummified for months), using one for cover and one bundled up for a pillow.

We were aghast. Somebody had actually been habitating in our uninhabitable house. Somebody had the nerve to *live* in our sixty rooms of unlivable splendor. Our first thought was to redouble our efforts and finish at least a few rooms so we could move in sooner. But then we realized it was useless. Moving into the house wouldn't help. Even if we had been there the night before, we would never have known about our uninvited guest if he hadn't left his nest behind. The bedrooms, after all, were half a football field away. Whole battalions of vagrants could be camped out in the far reaches of the house — hell, they could be throwing parties — and we wouldn't know it. Between shattered panes, splintered sashes, and now — thanks to my fervor for shiny brass — missing hardware, there was hardly a secure door or window in the place. If this had been New York, the squatters would have gone co-op by now.

The answer, of course, was a security system.

Based on the recommendation of a helpful neighbor, we called Mark, a young engineer from the Savannah River Site (aka the bomb plant) who moonlighted as a "home protection consultant." Surely, we figured, if the federal government trusted Mark to protect America's supply of tritium, a crucial ingredient in hydrogen bombs and a vital link in our nation's defense, Steve and I could trust him to make our home secure from sleepy vagrants.

But neither we nor the federal government had figured on one thing: Mark's principal assistant and fiancée, Marilyn, a fiercely attractive redhead with thick eye shadow, earrings the size of stirrups, a girlish laugh, and a venomous drawl.

In retrospect, we should have sensed trouble ahead the first time we visited Mark and Marilyn's "office" in the living room of her mother's mobile home. Mark was out of town, "on important government business," said Marilyn mysteriously, without taking her eyes off a huge coffee table spread with brochures for Caribbean honeymoon getaways. "He told me to give you these," she said as she threw a much smaller stack of brochures on various security systems in our general direction, returning immediately to her coffee table thoughts of sun, sand, and sex.

After a few minutes of studying the literature she gave us, we asked Marilyn if she would explain the difference between infrared and heat-sensitive motion detectors. Big mistake. She tapped her patent-leather pumps impatiently and reminded us that she was late for her dressmaker. And what about those motion detectors? "I'm having my great-grandmother's Victorian gown refitted," Marilyn added testily.

At another meeting, while we painstakingly tallied the number of windows and doors that needed to be wired, Marilyn described in rapturous detail the "icing angels" that would adorn her seven-tier wedding cake.

Surely, we figured, Mark would be more businesslike.

Perhaps. But not until after the wedding, after the seven-tier cake, and after two weeks of sun, sand, and sex in the Virgin Islands. (Thank God the Soviets didn't decide to launch a preemptive nuclear strike on the eve of Marilyn's wedding.) In fact, it wasn't until six weeks after we first contacted him about our nocturnal visitor and the urgent need for security that Mark even showed his face at Joye Cottage.

And then it was only to quit. "Now that I'm a married man," he announced, "I have to cut out these hobbies, like security consulting, and put my full energies into working my way up the job ladder at the [bomb] plant." (How many hours of Marilyn's coaching and confidence building had gone into that speech, I wondered.) But there was good news, too, he said. (We thought that *was* the good news.) He had sold his company to Joe Jackson, a reputable local businessman, who would honor Mark and Marilyn's commitment to make Joye Cottage secure.

But a few days later, it wasn't Mr. Jackson who showed up at the door, it was a guy in torn jeans, T-shirt, and turned-back baseball cap. He said his name was Glenn.

Glenn what?

"Just Glenn."

Just Glenn said he worked for Mr. Jackson; indeed, he was Mr. Jackson's *partner* in this new security venture, and it was he, not Mr. Jackson, who would actually install our system.

Glenn looked like Charles Manson, only less wholesome. Like Manson, he smiled a lot — in the same glazed, menacing way. Was this the man to deliver us from Aiken's criminal element? Steve tried to reassure me that a lot of people looked like that and smiled like that but they weren't all Charles Mansons. I found this less than reassuring.

But we needed the system.

So after a call to Mr. Jackson, we explained to "Just Glenn" what we needed done and handed him a twelve-hundred-dollar check as a down payment on the system. He smiled that worrisome smile and promised to be back the next morning to begin laying the miles of wire that the new system would require.

And that was the last we saw of him.

Several days passed before we called Mr. Jackson to ask what had happened to Just Glenn.

"Funny thang y'all should caull," said Mr. Jackson in that sugar-and-cream accent some southerners pour on, like honey on grits, as a last line of defense. "Ah'm afraid we got ourselves a smaull prob'm. I shur was meanin' ta caull y'all."

Right. "What kind of problem?"

"Well." Jackson hesitated. "Ya' see, Glenn, he done quit on me."

That didn't seem like such a problem. Glenn hadn't even started the job yet. We had lost only a few days. Surely we could make that up. Worse could happen, we reassured Mr. Jackson buoyantly.

"Well," said Mr. Jackson with a long pause. "Ah'm afraid it awready did. He done cashed yur check and kep' the money."

Now *that* was a problem. We would have to enlist the police to go after him. "Where is he now?" we demanded.

"He done disappeared," Jackson blurted, relieved to have the whole story out. "Left his wahf and two kids and jest disappeared."

For *twelve hundred dollars!* We didn't know whether to feel anger at Just Glenn for ripping us off, embarrassment at the barbed irony of being ripped off by the man we had paid to protect us, regret at having unwittingly provided the incentive for him to bolt his family — or guilt that we hadn't paid him enough to take the wife and kids along.

21.

Chicken-itza

Fortunately, we had a lot better luck finding the rest of the crew we needed to rescue W.C.'s winter palace from the insults of time.

Dave, the electrician, a transplanted Yankee like us, was the rock-star wannabe of the crew, an ambition that put his self-image in open warfare with his occupation. Dave owned a Corvette and yearned for a Harley but drove a truck by day and a van with two kids on the weekends. He wore wraparound sunglasses and modishly long ringlets of hair that just brushed the starched collar of his brown uniform, the one with the "Dave" patch over the pocket. He was both college-educated *and* smart, but aimed for a speaking style somewhere between Hulk Hogan and Jethro Bodine: "Hey, ain't we got none of them three-way dimmer switches?" The overall effect was persuasive but disorienting. (Imagine Robert De Niro doing a remake of *Gomer Pyle, USMC*.) The funny business stopped at the front door, however. Whatever else he was, Dave was a pro and a true wizard with Romex wire — five miles of which would eventually disappear like spaghetti down the gullet of Joye Cottage.

Then there was J.T., the plumber. I suppose every project has its J.T. What Rhett was to *Gone with the Wind*, what Billy was to *Billy Budd*, what Count Vronsky was to *Anna Karenina*, that's what J.T. was to Joye Cottage. Alabama born and bred, with high Cherokee cheekbones, powerful, taut hands and arms, and a slightly bowlegged walk, J.T. was the Marlboro Man with a wrench and plunger. There was something about the swagger in his stride, the preacherly musk in his voice, and the earnest perfectionism that he brought to installing silent flush toilets that made him seem almost a mythic figure — the apotheosis of the working man, the hero in a Steinbeck novel or Sturges movie, the central icon in a social realist painting. Women who visited the work site also invariably commented on his great tush.

The only workman on the site who seriously challenged J.T.'s preeminent machismo wasn't a man at all. *She* was a middle-aged woman who, in addition to keeping house for a husband and six kids, installed wiring for telephones, cable television, and computers. Her name was Darla, I think, or maybe Carla. I'm not sure because we just called her the

Telephone Lady. Years of scrambling up and down poles and crawling through attics and basements laying wire for the phone company had left her with short, bulldog arms and legs and the upper body of a gymnast. She, like J.T., walked with a bow in her legs and a swagger in her step and hooked her thumbs behind her belt buckle whenever she stopped long enough to talk. When we asked her if she could lay the wires for a stereo system along with all the others, she smacked her gum hard a few times before answering in a voice like Darth Vader's: "Damn straight. Do it all the time."

That was the last question we dared to ask her.

Bart Hutchinson, a young cabinetmaker and handyman with a sweet, round choirboy face and a foamy-mouthed rottweiler chained in the back of his truck, headed up the team of carpenters. Bart, unlike the dog, seemed friendly enough. Soon after arriving, he organized a regular weekly cookout during the Friday lunch break for everyone working on the house, skilled and unskilled alike — even the most unskilled of all, Steve and me. We would all sit around trading tall tales, boasts, and dirty jokes while Bart happily grilled steaks on an ancient backyard barbecue that he had rescued from the roadside somewhere.

Dressed in torn T-shirt, baggy camouflage pants, and the de rigueur black-mesh fishing cap, Bart always spoke with the spare, surly accent of rural southern youth. I learned later, however, that he wasn't as southern as I was (i.e., Mississippi mother, Georgia father). And he wasn't rural, either. He wasn't even American. The son of an English mother, Bart had spent the first sixteen years of his life in a British public school, learning Chaucer, drinking tea, and playing cricket with the boys in white. Such is the malleability of youth that when his family moved to South Carolina, his high school classmates needed less than a year to beat the British clean out of him. All that remained now were a few words like *smarmy* or *rubric* that slipped out every now and then in unguarded moments like the last bubbles from a sunken ship.

Bart was hardly the only one of our crew who turned out to be both less and more than he appeared. One day, I looked out the window and saw a heavyset man trundling across the yard, apparently headed for a tall ladder propped up against the side of the house. ("Heavyset" is something of a kindness here.) Who could this be? I wondered. The only visitor we were expecting was the roofer, a man named Andy Beaulieu, whom I had only spoken to over the phone. But this was no roofer. No man ever looked more earthbound.

Until he climbed the ladder.

I don't know how he did it. If I hadn't seen it with my own eyes, I never would have believed it. He didn't so much climb as ascend, as if on a wire. One minute he was planted on the ground, his big, red round face, like a half-melted Christmas candle, staring up the ladder in what looked like sadness that his climbing days were over; then, in a twinkling, he was on the roof, testing the rotten shingles (and the strength of the rafters), a redneck Santa Claus in a black-mesh fishing cap.

It was, indeed, Andy Beaulieu, as I discovered when I clambered up the ladder after him. Only he pronounced it "Balloo." And his neck was, indeed, red — the deepest shade of red I ever saw — from all those hours of rooftop work under a Carolina sun. Born in Sylvania, a little town on the Georgia side of the Savannah River, Andy came on like a bad cliché, the worst nightmare of every Yankee who ever took the wrong exit off I-95 or 85 or 75 on the way to Disney World and ended up in a town called Sparta or Florence or Opelika. It was all there: the big gut, the casual bigotry, and a drawl so thick it acted like a heavy net, tangling every sentence into a writhing mass of words struggling to break free.

I asked him once what he did when he wasn't repairing roofs, expecting to hear something about cars or guns or maybe women. Instead: "Ah ten' mah orchids."

Orchids?

"Mah favrits are the Cattleyas," he says, rubbing his stomach in what I took to be a gesture of pride, "they's the big white ones with the purple throats. Most of thems comes outta Hawaiiah. Mah wahf, on th'other hand, she likes them cybiniums. For a long tahm, Ah was in this orchid society, but Ah just had too many thangs ta do."

Thangs like what?

Like grooming his prizewinning German shepherds. They had already won several blue ribbons at dog shows. "We lost the first one when she was in whelp with puppies," he lamented. "Then thar's this male we're showin'. He finished thard in the Nationals in Atlanta."

Anythang else?

"Layin' down rubber on asphalt," says Andy with a chuckle, and I think we've finally come around to the predictable car talk — four-wheelers and monster trucks and the rest. But no. "I was racin' one a mah motorcycles," says Andy, all 220-plus pounds of him. "I got eight Triumphs.

Mah last one Ah bought was a 'seventy-two. That one Ah bought nyew — Ah'm workin on that sucker now."

A few weeks later, after Andy had finished laying only about half of the acre of new shingles the house needed, he asked to take a week off "for a trip." Not having learned my lesson yet, I immediately assumed a hunting trip (the deer season had just begun) or maybe shrimping off the coast or trout fishing in the Georgia mountains. Something with the camouflage crowd. But no. Andy was heading for the slopes. Aspen. "Every yar now for twelve yars," he said. "Same hotel, same slopes, same people, every yar." (I tried, unsuccessfully, to imagine Andy on skis.) In the spring, he said, he always heads south to Mexico. This year he plans to visit the ruins at "Chicken-itza."

Just goes to show, you can't tell a redneck by his red neck.

22.

Michelangelo in White

Within six weeks, Andy and his fellow workers had turned Joye Cottage into a ruin. Like the proverbial patient who only gets sicker in the hospital, our once-beautiful, if dilapidated, home began to look like the set for a "day after" docudrama, reduced by the combined ministrations of carpenters, electricians, plumbers, and Mordia's demolition squad to a skeletal shadow of its former glory.

To make the massive jobs of rewiring and replumbing "easier," Bart had persuaded us to remove every square inch of old plaster and lath from all but a few rooms — a task akin to tearing down and carting away the Great Wall of China, bucket of rubble by bucket of rubble. In the process, the laborers filled up and hauled away twenty or thirty Dumpsters the size of railroad cars and created a cloud of plaster dust sure to affect weather patterns over the Southeast for years to come. When all that dust eventually settled back to earth, it coated everything in a shroud of white powder as fine and intractable as talc. Workers emerged from the rubble at quitting time like bands of ghosts from the House of Usher. Every time we tried to sweep the stuff up, we just stirred up another giant cloud of it.

Just when it looked like there was no escape, just when it seemed that we would be living with bare studs and breathing plaster dust for the rest of our lives, a miracle happened. We found a plasterer.

In an earlier era, that wouldn't have been such a cause for celebration. Like brass, plaster was once the building material of choice in America's houses, and not just on Easy Street. From Marvin Gardens to Park Place, plasterers were as common as carpenters, and as cheap. Then, in the 1960s, Sheetrock (aka drywall, aka plasterboard) hit the building industry like hurricane Hugo, and American interiors were never the same again. Gone were walls you couldn't put your foot through or hear your neighbors through. Gone too were all those intricate plaster cornices and moldings and medallions that wouldn't stick to drywall — gone or, even worse, "reinterpreted" in pressed wood, plastic, and Styrofoam. Only historical fanatics and addled purists bothered with plaster anymore. Too much time, too much mess. And besides, all the good plasterers were dying off. Plastering had become the Latin of construction. As long as a few old coots could be found to fix the stuff when it broke (as when the real Hugo swept through Charleston, the same month we moved to Aiken), who wanted to learn a dying trade?

Eugene Fisher was one of those old coots. He materialized the first day dressed all in white: white shirt, white pants, even white hair. A vision in white. We learned later that, in the old days, plasterers always wore white to distinguish themselves from the other trades on a site. It was a matter of pride and professionalism. For Eugene, it still was.

Born in nearby Augusta, Eugene had started plastering when he was thirteen, he told us. (He wouldn't divulge his age, but he talked about Roosevelt and Truman in the same breath as Reagan and Bush, so we figured him for sixty at least.) He said it had taken him four years to learn his trade. At first, his mentors would only let him lay on the "brown coat," a thick layer of coarse, cementlike plaster applied directly to the lath, the heavy metal mesh that is screwed to the studs. From there he graduated to "skim coat" — another undercoat — and then finally, after more years of practice, to "white coat," the thin layer of finish plaster that when applied right is smooth and flat as glass. "Back in my day," he would say — everything before 1960 was "his day" — "when ya first done finish coat, ya only done closets. I probably did closets for a year or two before they let me white-coat any *rooms*."

Eugene had spent most of his prime plastering years in Florida, during the first wave of construction along Ocean Drive in Miami Beach. He had worked on all the big hotels there — the Fontainebleau, the Flamingo, the Doral — laying on acres of beautiful white plaster, "most of which they painted pink," he would note ruefully.

Around Bart's Friday barbecues and pretty much anywhere, anytime anybody would listen, Eugene spun stories from the threads of his past. His favorite was any story about "the syndicate" — a sinister, mob-related group that, according to Eugene, ran the construction trades in south Florida. "Everyone I worked for was connected to them," he would say. "Hell, *all* the construction in Florida was connected to them." He told one story about a guy named Paul who was the "taker" on one project; he "took" 5 percent of what everybody working there was making. "And if ya didn't pay him," Eugene recalled, "ya didn't have a job. It was that simple. When he first came on the project, he had holes in his shoes. I know that for a fact. Then, overnight, he built hisself a house that cost two hundred fifty thousand dollars. In three years, he was a millionaire."

Then one day Paul turned up dead, along with his wife — shot nine times on a road in the Everglades, then run over with his own car. "Construction was a rough game in Florida," Eugene would editorialize. A few days later, the police came around with an artist's composite of the chief suspect in the case and asked Eugene if he recognized it.

"Yeah," said Eugene, ever the perfectionist, "only ya don't have him exactly right." In fact, the picture was of Eugene's chief lather, a man named Sam — "a terrific guy," according to Eugene. And yes, come to think of it, Sam had been missing from work the last few days.

Eugene hated to lose a good lather, but eventually he located Sam, coaxed him out of hiding, and persuaded him to turn himself in. At least that's the way Eugene told the story. And told it, and told it. Nor was that the end of it. (Eugene's stories rarely ended where you expected them to. In fact, they rarely ended at all.) As it turned out, Sam had not only murdered the taker and his wife (a crime for which everyone but the police seemed willing to forgive him) but had also stolen money from the taker's apartment — syndicate money — a far more serious offense. Convinced that Sam had told Eugene where the money was hidden, the syndicate *capo* made Eugene an offer he couldn't refuse: "If ya don't tell us where the money is, we'll kill you."

Did he tell?

Eugene would always smile, lift his cap, and run his big hand over his white hair before answering enigmatically: "I'll never tell."

With his stories about the syndicate (or political corruption in Augusta, another favorite topic) and an unending patter of backwoods bons mots ("Stick with me, and I'll have ya fartin' through silk"), Eugene could be the kind of person you hate sitting next to on a plane. But once he got a trowel in his hand, he was an artist.

His raw materials were nothing more than buckets of plaster hauled in from a rickety old mixer outside and dumped on a big table in the middle of the room. From there, Eugene would slap a heavy scoop of the goop onto his mortarboard — his palette. Every stage of the job required a different skill. Brown coat had to be applied with enough pressure to push the plaster through the metal mesh of the lath — but not all the way through. It also had to be laid on thickly or thinly to compensate for any major irregularities in the wall: out of square, out of level, out of line.

(Hardly a room at Joye Cottage didn't require some correcting.) As a result, it might be only three-quarters of an inch thick in one place, three or four inches in another. If a room was in particularly bad shape, it could consume massive quantities of brown coat. The stuff came in fifty-pound bags to which the mixer added fifty pounds of water per bag, and Eugene sometimes went through twenty bags in a single room. That's a ton of plaster. Literally. And all of it applied, trowel by trowel, by Eugene.

The skim coat had to cover the rough brown coat and still achieve something like a finished surface. It was both a first pass at smoothness and a last chance at flatness.

And then came the white coat, the final coat, the finish coat. Perfection. Like everything else, it started off as just a bucket of white plaster dumped on the table. Eugene would shape it into a ring, fill the ring with water, then mix in the gauging powder that made the white coat dry firmer and faster. Much faster. Once mixed, the stuff would harden in forty-five minutes — no mistakes, no breaks, no excuses. Anything not used in forty-five minutes had to be thrown out. It was an unforgiving medium. The first time we watched Eugene apply white coat, his burly frame balanced on a shaky latticework of scaffold as he reached for the ceiling over his head, we had visions of Michelangelo madly painting the ceiling of the Sistine Chapel, forced to execute each day's imagery before the plaster dried.

Eugene could walk the length of a room — twenty, thirty, forty feet — stepping over lumber and buckets, with his trowel high over his head or down below his knees, he could walk a shaky gangplank of scaffolding with his trowel against the ceiling and leave a trail of plaster as smooth and flat and flawless as a mirror.

White coating separated the real plasterers from the mere stucco men — the young bucks who applied concrete to the exteriors of million-dollar tract mansions in Atlanta or, even worse, in bigger projects, *sprayed* it on. Eugene couldn't imagine how anybody who used a spray gun could call himself a plasterer. Plastering was all in the feel. Everything a plasterer needed to know was communicated from the wall, up through the wooden handle of his trowel, and into his hand. Like any master plasterer, Eugene knew in an instant if the wall was out of level. He could feel the bumps and valleys (the "humps and hollers," he called them) that even a level couldn't detect. If his trowel wavered or dipped or swerved so much as a millimeter, Eugene knew it. He felt it. Hell, he could plaster in the dark.

23.

The Search for Security

Every day that Eugene worked his messy magic, another wall went up. Every few days, another room was reclaimed from the forest of studs and foliage of rubble. Finally, we had turned the corner. Finally, the house was looking *better* every day, not worse. We could see the light at the end of the tunnel. By all rights, we should have been thrilled, delighted, ecstatic.

Wrong.

Of course, we were thrilled to see rooms again. It had been so long we had almost forgotten what the inside looked like. But every one of Eugene's perfectly smooth, immaculately white walls reminded us that something still wasn't done: the security system. Every finished wall was one less wall we could run security wires through easily. Every day we felt like Errol Flynn racing to escape the castle before the portcullis clamped down and trapped him inside — or, for a more up-to-date image, how about Indiana Jones in front of the rolling boulder. We didn't dare stop Eugene's inexorable progress (I'm not sure we could have), but if we were going to wire the house for security, we had to do something. And quickly.

In desperation, we gave Mr. Jackson another chance to make good on our contract. This time, at least, the man he sent to our door didn't look like a mass murderer. More like an accountant. Even more encouraging, he had two names: Mike and Martinez. "That's MAR-ti-nez," he was quick to inform us, "not Mar-TI-nez. It's German, not Hispanic."

We were happy for the clarification, we told him, but really didn't care what his name or ancestry was. We just wanted our security system installed.

He did not take our indifference lightly. A look of great consternation came over his face as he gravely mulled it over in search of a latent ethnic slur.

Mike — we decided to avoid the last name altogether — eventually did get to work on the security system, drilling holes in door frames and windowsills, and unspooling reel after reel of wire from one end of the house to the other. In just three weeks, more than twenty-five thousand feet of the stuff disappeared down the black hole of the basement stairs — almost five *miles* of wire.

And then, almost simultaneously, his life unraveled.

We could tell within a week of Mike's arrival that something was wrong. Every day he came into work looking a little more disturbed, disheveled, and distracted than the day before. Finally, after two weeks of watching this Dorian Gray progression, I ventured to ask softly, "Is anything wrong?"

Big mistake. Mike burst into tears and explained in one heaping, dripping pile of words his entire life story — computer nerd marries high school sweetheart, has two kids, gets a good job at the bomb plant — and then, just when life seems perfect, she walks out on him. Another huge, leonine sob. Worse still, she says she wants sole custody of the kids.

The next day, Mike didn't show up for work. I figured he was just taking a day to recover. Maybe he felt he had revealed too much, especially for a German. But he didn't come in the next day, either, or the next, or the next. And all the while Eugene's juggernaut of plaster and patter continued to roll through Joye Cottage, simultaneously slathering up walls and driving his bucket-toting helpers to suicidal distraction.

Finally, on the third day, we called Mr. Jackson.

"Funny thang y'all should caull," said Mr. Jackson in that same irritating accent. "Ah'm afraid we got ourselves a smaull prob'm. I shur was meanin' ta caull y'all."

Again. "What kind of problem?"

"Well." Jackson hesitated. "Ya' see, Mike, he done disappeared on me."

"Disappeared?"

"You know," Jackson explained carefully. "Gone."

I explained that I knew what *disappeared* meant. "Gone where?"

"I just was talkin' to the *po*lice about that," said Jackson. "Seems nobody has a *clue* where he ran off to."

That didn't seem like such a problem. Sad, maybe, but not a problem. Mike had accomplished a lot in two weeks, and we had missed only a few days. Surely we could make that up. It could be worse, we heard ourselves reassuring Mr. Jackson again.

"Well," said Mr. Jackson with a long pause. "It is. Mike didn't go alone. He absconded his kids, too. He was set on gettin' 'em away from his wife."

Now *that* was a problem.

"So you and me ain't the only ones lookin' for him. His wife, the *po*lice, the courts, they're all out after him. And now they think he crossed the state line, the FBI is huntin' for him, too. He's in a heap'a trouble."

"And what about our security system?" I ventured to ask.

"Funny thang . . . ," Mr. Jackson drawled.

24.

Country Life

Three months after work began, we were finally able to move into one wing of the house (actually one part of one wing: three rooms and a bathroom). Paradoxically, it was the wing that had been abandoned the longest — almost from the time it was built. It was one of the two wings W.C. had added for his sons, specifically the one for his younger son, William Payne. But when Willie renounced his father in favor of his uncle Oliver's millions, W.C. closed the wing up. And so it remained for almost a hundred years, more or less unoccupied, a monument to hurt and anger and family betrayal. Not surprisingly, generations of Whitney children, who grew up running through its big, abandoned rooms, dubbed it the Spooky Wing.

Eugene, the runaway boulder, had done his thing, and Dave, the electrician, had hooked up just enough power for lights, shavers, TV, computer, and cranky baseboard heaters. At night, we felt like squatters, huddled in our little lighted corner surrounded by room upon room of empty darkness. At night, the house was at its biggest. We would stand at the window in the sitting room, which, on a moonlit night, provided a spectacular panorama of the courtyard and a big square of starry night sky that we fancied "ours" because it was completely framed by the house and could not be seen, at precisely that angle anyway, from any other spot on earth.

On nights like that, the house seemed very big, the dark windows very dark, and the space behind them very forbidding. And that was before Steve went to Texas to begin the research for our next book, leaving me more alone than ever. There I sat, alone on the couch in the sitting room, surrounded by the empty vastness of Joye Cottage, watching *Cops* on Fox, thinking about Steve and the book he was researching — a true-crime thriller about a murderer who broke into a huge mansion one night and started killing people.

Suddenly, through the fog of TV sedation, I heard something that sounded like bells. Was it on the TV? The image of two New Orleans policemen berating a suspect in the station house lockup was flickering across the screen. Bells in a New Orleans police station?

Seconds later I heard it again. On the TV was a commercial for Safeguard deodorant soap. It wasn't the TV. Out of the corner of my eye, I saw a brief, unusual flicker of light in the courtyard. The beam of a flashlight was bouncing crazily off the side of the ballroom wing. There was a dark shape moving around the pool in the center of the courtyard. It was low to the ground — and it had four legs. A dog, then two dogs. The ringing sound returned. It was coming from the dogs. They had bells on their collars.

Suddenly something began to rise up from underneath the window, just on the other side of the glass, maybe six inches from me. I recoiled violently, stumbling back against the couch, but the shape continued to rise, as if levitating. The first thing I saw was a black baseball cap with the letters "S-L-E-D" printed across it. I had no idea what it meant. The first thing that came to mind was "Rosebud." Next to emerge was a face — a stern face with a moustache. Next came his black, padded vest, and finally, a long black metal gun. I recognized it from the movies as the kind of assault rifle SWAT teams carry.

Suddenly, the courtyard was full of caps — caps and guns, dogs and bouncing flashlight beams. I went to the nearest door, where another man in vest and heavy artillery informed me that a convict had escaped while being transported. In the process, he had shot an officer in the foot — an especially heinous assault because the wounded officer was a star on the division's championship basketball team. SLED, it now came back to me, was an acronym for State Law Enforcement Division, South Carolina's heavily armed answer to the FBI. "Keep your doors locked," the man in the vest called out as he ran to catch up with the dogs.

I watched the last of the SLED caps scramble across the courtyard, then turned back to the TV, where the New Orleans police were breaking up a barroom fight on Bourbon

Street. A lot of yelling — rough, rude language perforated by those little holes in the soundtrack where the juiciest words should be. "You ——ing ——," one of the bar patrons was yelling at a female bystander who was, apparently, the one who had called the cops, "your ——ing ——'s gonna get ——ed tonight!" Or something to that effect.

Then, just as the brawlers were being led away, the yelling started up again. Only this time without the holes: "Get the fuck down here . . ." "We'll blow your fucking head off . . ." There must have been five or ten voices this time, all male, their angry shouts punctuated by barking dogs. I pressed the mute button. The yelling continued. *It was coming from outside.* I went to the french doors that opened onto the porch. The magnolia tree just beyond the stately white columns was surrounded by SLED caps and dogs: dogs barking, men shouting. Mean, coarse, angry shouting. More like barking. Men with guns and dogs with bells, all barking up into the big-leafed magnolia.

In the tree, maybe ten feet off the ground, something moved. The fugitive was there. In *our* tree. They climbed after him, grabbed the cuff of his pants, and pulled ferociously. He tumbled through the branches and fell awkwardly to the ground with a heavy thud. The dogs went crazy. So did the men. They kicked him and cursed at him even as a half dozen guns were pointed at him. As he covered his face to ward off the blows, they wrestled him onto his stomach, handcuffed his hands behind his back, then dragged him to his feet. The dogs howled victoriously.

Ten years in New York City and I had never seen a gun drawn in anger. No muggings, not even a close call. I turned back to the TV, where the New Orleans cops were settling

what appeared to be a perfectly harmless domestic dispute. Who needed television?

Led by the triumphant dogs, the cops took their prize back through the courtyard toward the street. As I watched from the big window, I saw the fugitive, dazed and chastened, lift his head and look around. He took in the whole panorama: the two long wings with their classical porches on either side and the hundred-foot veranda spread in front of him.

Was it my imagination, or was he smiling? Was it my paranoia, or was the first thing he would tell his cell mates: "You won't believe the house where they caught me"?

25.

The People I Killed

The next day at Bart's Friday barbecue, the story of my brush with the law was the talk of the work site — although not the kind of talk I expected.

"Damn, I wish he'd climb up *my* tree," said Manny, a member of Bart's carpentry crew with a face like a maniacal Cabbage Patch doll. "I'd'a' blowed his fuckin' head off!"

Animated by this turn in the conversation, Bart looked up from the grill and demanded to know how *exactly* Manny would have accomplished that particular feat.

With a worrisome smile, Manny ran to his truck and pulled from behind the seat a bulky, black, fearsome-looking gun.

I recognized it instantly. *It was the same gun I had seen the night before.* Only this time it wasn't in the hands of a SLED commando; it was in the hands of a manic-depressive carpenter filled with rages and grudges.

"Where'd you get that?" I couldn't help asking.

"Oh, sheeut," said Manny, "you can get these things anywhere."

And, indeed, you can. A few days later, I was strolling down the aisle of the local, inevitable Wal-Mart and sure enough, there behind the small kitchen appliances, between hardware and house supplies, was the Murder and Mayhem department. Guns, guns, guns. Rack upon rack of them. Big guns, little guns, starter guns, ender guns. Guns for the purse and guns, like Manny's, for the pickup. Enough guns to resupply the Iraqi army. Accompanying these, of course, was everything the modern American hunter household needed: the latest in camouflage-fatigue wear and designer ammunition, combat boots, and, of course, for hunters who feared the deer might arm themselves, flak jackets.

The M & M department was crowded. Because of the hour, it was mostly women at this arms bazaar; some had brought their kids. The little tykes seemed particularly interested in the assault rifles on the wall behind the counter and the big handguns under glass. I watched one mother in a pink nylon winter coat as she held her infant and eyed a case of automatic pistols. What did her shopping list look like? I wondered.

four 100-watt bulbs
three six-packs of Tab

two boxes of Pampers
one Uzi
2,000 rounds of ammo

The very same day as my trip to the Wal-Mart of Death, the subject of guns came up again at Bart's lunchtime barbecue and confab. It began, as usual, with the traditional exchange of hunters' boasts: Who shot from the farthest, under the harshest conditions, with the least sleep, after drinking the most alcohol, and inflicted the ugliest wound on the biggest buck (the one with the most "points" on its antlers), etc., etc., ad nauseam. I hadn't heard anything like it since my Mississippi grandfather gave me a .22 for my twelfth birthday and, thinking he was doing my manhood a great favor, dragged me into the woods at six in the morning.

It wasn't until another member of Bart's crew, a young man named Bill, started talking about his two-year-old daughter, Tiffany, that I began to get queasy. For lack of a son, it seems, Bill had started taking little Tiffany deer hunting with him. This, of course, was a feminist twist on the traditional my-son-will-be-a-better-hunter-than-yours-because-he-started-earlier boast, and the assembled workmen, recognizing it as such, nodded appreciatively. Well, bragged Bill, little Tiffany was so delighted by this new activity with her father that she had taken to searching the highways for deer whenever they rode in the car together.

More appreciative bobbing of heads. How sweet.

"Whenever she sees one," Bill reported with obvious paternal pride, "she turns to me and says, 'Daddy, look! A deer, a deer! *Kill* the deer, Daddy! *Kill* the deer!'" More nodding and smiles of appreciation all around.

For days afterward, I was haunted by the image of a doe-eyed Bambi caught in the headlights of Bill's pickup and the gleeful laughter of a little two-year-old girl pressing her chubby finger against the windshield in bright-eyed wonder and squealing, "*Kill* the deer, Daddy! *Kill* the deer!"

Manny, who was obviously the most animated by this subject, jumped in with a story about the time he and Bill foiled a robbery attempt. "These two black fellas — kids — come into this store where me and Bill stopped on the way back from shrimping on the coast. They said some things to the lady behind the counter, so me and Bill went to our trucks and got our shotguns. Well, hell, as soon as they seen us comin' back in loaded, they split out the door. So me and Bill hightailed it after 'em, shootin' as we ran."

"You mean you *shot* at them as they were running away?" I asked incredulously. I noticed that I was the only one who seemed in the slightest alarmed by this.

"Naw," said Manny, "just in the air — to scare 'em."

Much more alarming to everyone else was what followed. "While me and Bill is chasin' 'em," Manny continued, "the lady behind the counter calls the sheriff. So what happens? When we come back, the cops arrive and they hassle *us!*"

Much grumbling and cursing and gnashing of teeth. "What the hell for?" someone protested.

"*For shootin' off our guns!*" More cursing and grumbling. "The sheriff's givin' me and Bill a whole lotta shit, when you'd think they'd pay more attention to the two guys that held up the store."

Did the black guys show a gun? I wondered out loud. Did they actually threaten the lady or demand money?

"That's not the fuckin' point," Manny growled.

Ah. I decided to let the subject drop.

But then Eugene, who always had to have a better story than anyone else, and usually did, jumped in: "Well, there was this time me and my wife was driving out of the parking lot at the mall and a young guy knocks on the window and tells me to roll it down. He points this knife at me, this *big* knife" — Eugene put down his sandwich and held his hands about three feet apart — "and tells me to give him my wallet. I say, 'Okay.' I mean, my wife's there and all. And so I say, 'Let me just get it for ya.' So I reach down and pull out my thirty-eight. You can imagine the surprised look on his face when I shoot him."

Yes.

"Anyway, so he keels over. Dead."

"What did the police do?" I asked. Even in South Carolina, even when the killee pulls a knife on the killer, even when the killee is black and the killer is white, one would think that killing a person would entail certain, well, complications.

"Ya can't imagine the shit they put me through," said Eugene with indignation verging on outrage.

"The *cops?*" It was Manny's turn to be incredulous.

"Hell, no, not the cops," said Eugene. "They understand about self-protection, and the Second Amendment, and all that stuff." (I was glad somebody did.) "It was the guy's *family*. They hired a damnlawyer" — a single word, as he said it — "and sued me."

"What for?" someone demanded.

"Hell, you name it. I don't know. I spent close to twenty thousand dollars and three years in and out of court defendin' myself on that one."

Everyone agreed that this was a travesty of justice, that the legal system protected criminals and not their law-abiding victims, and especially that all damnlawyers ought to be taken out, scolded, and shot.

All this talk of shooting put Manny in mind of a question. "Who else here has shot somebody?" he asked as he put up his hand.

Half a dozen hands went up — out of a total of ten workmen.

Manny seemed pleased. I was shocked, and it showed. "How many of you own guns?" I asked, openmouthed.

Every hand went up.

"How many bring guns with you to work in the morning?"

Five hands went up before someone muttered, "Does it count if it's in your truck?" When I said yes, two more hands shot up. Someone else wanted "extra credit" for having two guns in his truck. Manny had *three*. Mordia reached under his coat and pulled out a .38 magnum to show that while he may not have been the most heavily armed person present, he was certainly the most readily armed. Manny and Bill went stiff. I was still wrestling with the realization that the work site was an armed camp.

But the founding fathers would have been proud. If that invasion long promised by the NRA came in the next few months, Joye Cottage would be either the safest place in the Southeast — or the next Alamo.

26.

The Search for Security, Continued

With criminals literally falling from the trees and small children screaming for blood, the lack of security loomed suddenly very large. What was it about installing the security system at Joye Cottage that caused people to disappear? If it wasn't Just Glenn escaping from his family, it was Mike MAR-ti-nez escaping *with* his family. Mr. Jackson shoveled on the apologies and turned up the color dial on his accent ("I tell y'all, I'm jest jam up 'bout this!"), but Eugene's trowel stopped for no man, and the walls were closing in around us.

Figuring, I guess, that the third time was a charm, Mr.

Jackson sent us Randy, a sour, scrawny man with a perennial five-o'clock shadow, who was anything but charming. Among Randy's many problems, the most extravagant was his problem with alcohol. The very first time we directed him to the basement to inspect the unfinished tangle of wires left by Mike MAR-ti-nez, he took one step, lost his footing, and tumbled down the stairs into the darkness. After a long silence, we heard a blurred but unbowed voice: "Absolutely no problem."

From that point, it was all downhill.

For three days, Randy virtually disappeared into the basement, no doubt familiarizing himself with the system, we figured. When he finally emerged, Steve cornered him and demanded to know if he could finish installing the system in good time.

"Absolutely no problem," said Randy, waving his arms too widely in a reassuring gesture that was anything but reassuring.

A week later, Steve cornered him again. What portion of the system had he finished? Steve wanted to know. Randy looked shocked. "The impedance factor in some of these wires is too high for the amperage of the voltmeter" (or something like that), he muttered indignantly. "And these working conditions is frigging impossible."

"Well, are you almost done?" Steve pressed.

Randy sucked in his gut, then exhaled a cloud of toxic gas. "Absolutely no problem."

By now, Randy's breath wasn't the only thing about him that reeked. We had noticed when he started work that he smelled ripe. A week later, he was way past ripe. Was he as far behind on the job as he was in his personal hygiene? we wondered. Every time Steve tried to pry a schedule out of him, he would wave his arms unsteadily and insist, "Absolutely no problem."

Then, one evening, in a routine reconnaissance of the house after everyone had left, Steve found Randy sitting on an empty spool in a dark corner of the basement, with a bottle in his hand.

Not knowing what to say, Steve went into default mode: concern. "Is everything all right?" he asked.

That was too much for poor Randy. He was expecting a tongue-lashing, a temperance lecture, or a boot in the rear. Or all three. But not kindness. He burst into tears.

Then, after much weeping and wailing, came the story.

He was a failure at love. He had fallen in love with a girl he met at his favorite bar, the Roundabout, only to find out later that she was a lesbian. Then, on the rebound, he had fallen in love with another girl who hung out at the Roundabout. Then, just the week before, he had learned that she, too, preferred sex with other women. Randy let out a sob that filled the basement. "Is there something about me," he wailed, "that turns women queer?"

Oh, God, thought Steve as he waded into a basic science lesson on the probable genetic origins of homosexuality, will this security system ever get finished?

Part Three **Getting Acquainted**

27.

Celebrity

Imagine our surprise, after years of ice-cube-tray anonymity in a Manhattan high-rise, when, soon after our arrival in Aiken, we fetched our copy of the local newspaper from the driveway and found our picture on the front page, above the fold no less, accompanied by the banner headline: "BEST-SELLER AUTHORS SETTLE IN AIKEN, BUY JOYE COTTAGE."

Two of America's most popular new writers, who are shooting up the best-seller lists with their true-life tales about violence,

*have purchased the historic 60-room Joye Cottage and will use
the rambling mansion as both a residence and workplace.*

Questions of accuracy aside — "America's most popular
new writers"??? — we came to realize that making the
front page of a small-town paper wasn't exactly the same as
getting a good table at Spago's. Over the next year, the front
page would feature a vegetable contest as often as the war
in the Gulf and lavish front-page pictures of the annual
"ugly shorts" contest.

Word of the new "celebrities" in town soon reached the
highest levels of government.

Dear Mr. Naifeh and Mr. Smith:

*I would like to take this opportunity to welcome you to the
city of Aiken. . . .*

*It certainly is exciting to have such distinguished writers
join our community.*

Strom Thurmond

We were feeling quite warm and inflated about our new
status until Wilma, our real estate agent, told us that the distinguished and very senior senator from South Carolina
sent similar letters to every new resident who had demon-
strated (by buying a big house, for example) an ability to
contribute to his never-ending reelection campaign.

Sometimes it was hard to tell who was the bigger
celebrity, us or the house. Soon after we arrived, papers and
magazines in the area began running old file photos of Joye

Cottage, often on the slenderest of excuses. The *Augusta Chronicle* illustrated an article on renovation self-help tips with an aerial shot of our sixty-room house, looking especially immense and daunting. *Augusta* magazine graciously — and optimistically — voted ours the year's "Best Renovation" when work had barely begun.

It wasn't long before the tour buses began lumbering our way, tearing up the clay street as they inched past our driveway, faces and cameras pressed against the windows. Close behind came a steady stream of curious, mostly well-intentioned gawkers. I walked out on the porch one day to find three Canadian tourists high in the big oak tree out back. When I asked what they were doing, they insisted, somewhat indignantly, that they were trying to get a good picture.

When our Pollock biography was finally released in December 1989, only a few months after we arrived in Aiken, Steve and I managed to edge our way ahead of the house in the celebrity sweepstakes. For a while, at least. In addition to reviews and feature stories in all the major regional papers, we hosted a reporter from the *Washington Post*, who wrote a flattering (and very perceptive) front-page article for that paper's style section, once again featuring a picture of the two authors standing in front of "their new home in the South." Then, one afternoon in January 1990, our fellow Aikenites were astonished to turn on their televisions and see "the boys" — the phrase applied to us by almost everyone in town, one that somehow became less irritating as we passed forty — being interviewed by Phil Donahue.

After that, we noticed a change in the way people treated us. Even the way they looked at us. In the fertilizer store, we went to the register to pay for the ton of horse manure we had picked out, and the lady behind the counter greeted us with a big grin. Steve started to give her our address so they could deliver the, uh, stuff, but she cut him off with a wave of her hand. "I know who you are," she said very sweetly, kind of like Kathy Bates in *Misery*. "And I know where you live, too."

Through it all, we tried to keep in mind what happened to our friend Michael, an accomplished painter, who tended to think of himself as a star just because he looked like one, more or less. One evening, when Michael was promenading down Lexington Avenue, he passed a knot of young women, all wide eyes and heavy makeup. New Jersey, he figured.

"Look!" one of the girls squealed to her friends, flapping her wrist in excitement as Michael ambled by. "There's *somebody!*"

Four women, eight eyes, locked onto Michael's aquiline profile as it passed. After just a few moments of fierce attention, though, the spell broke. "Oh, no," said one of the women, turning away in crestfallen disgust. "It's *nobody!*"

I was reminded of that incident one day when Steve and I were grocery shopping at Kroge's. The checkout lady, a wide-hipped woman with a great mound of hair topped by one small, red barrette, like a cherry on a sundae, looked at us with sparkling blue eyes and profound curiosity. I was sure that she "recognized" us. "Don't you two have horses?" she asked, giving us a coy smile and the word *horses* about seven syllables.

"Horses?"

"Well, aren't y'all the two famous riders?"

"That's *writers*," said Steve, "not *riders*."

"Oh," said the woman, recovering her composure as she reached for the last of our groceries. "Never mind."

28.

The One with Legs

None of the hoopla, however — if it can be called that — had much effect on the crew working at the house. Not, that is, until our newfound celebrity landed us an invitation to judge the Miss South Carolina Beauty Contest. Of course, as conscientious feminists we had no choice but to turn the offer down cold.

That was before we made the mistake of sharing the invitation with the crew.

The news hit like a bombshell. Not since rumors of the Whitney Silver sent everyone scrambling for their shovels had we seen such enthusiasm. Thanks mostly to Mordia

Grant, who was positively apoplectic with envy, news of our spectacular good fortune spread quickly through the largely male ranks of subcontractors, suppliers, delivery drivers, and salesclerks who followed our sixty-room folly from the sidelines. Soon we couldn't pull into a gas station or stand in line at the grocery store without some adolescent male (of whatever age) grinning knowingly and offering some variation on "It's a tough job, but somebody's gotta do it." Wink, wink, nod, nod.

In the end, we bent to the pressure.

The pageant was held in Myrtle Beach, South Carolina's answer to Atlantic City (with discount stores standing in for casinos). There, at an all-the-fish-and-chicken-you-can-eat get-acquainted party, we met our fellow judges for the first time. The unlikely group included a retired Broadway showgirl, now an elegant, sixtyish lady from Charleston; an attractive young couple who labored somewhere in the fashion-industry food chain and insisted they were taking part in such a lowbrow entertainment only to find models for their runway shows; two twentysomething men, chosen apparently for no better reason than that they looked terrific in suits; and, finally, two older gentlemen — one white-haired, the other bald — who took great pains to let the rest of us know that they had judged dozens of similar contests.

The bald one was particularly eager to share his accumulated wisdom. "Remember this one thing," he said as his lips searched what was left of a piece of fried chicken for overlooked morsels. "This ain't the Miss America contest. There ain't no talent competition." I, for one, found that deeply disappointing. No baton twirling, no ventriloquism, no maracas? "This is jest a pretty-gal contest," he continued, licking his fingers. "All we gotta do is pick the gal who can go on and win the Miss USA title. And she won't win if she ain't pretty and she ain't tall. Between a short gal and a tall gal, always pick 'em tall. A gal jest can't win the Miss USA title if she ain't tall and leggy." The profoundness of this insight seemed to give him special pleasure. He stuck his thumb in his mouth for one long, last lick and eased it out slowly. "Yes, sir," he concluded, punctuating the point with a final, authoritative smack. "Pick the one with legs."

We convened at the pageant venue, a small community college outside Myrtle Beach, for our first look at the assembled legs. To help us keep score, we were given a photo guide to the contestants, like a college face book, in which all the girls — they were *never* referred to as women — were pictured and their sponsors listed: "Mom and Dad," "Aunt Mildred," "Cousin Betty Sue." In some cases, contestants were sponsored by local businesses: "Gloria's Bridals," "Fresh Scent Florists," "Bob's Tire Repair Shop," etc.

What exactly *is* the role of a sponsor? I asked one of the *éminences grises*, the one with hair.

"Why, hell, these gals have to pay to get into this contest, you know. How else could the pageant make money? Sometimes the family pays, sometimes a local business pays. That's how it works."

Did the contestants have to meet any other requirements? I wondered. Work their way up from regional contests? Pass some sort of preliminary selection process? Submit their pictures?

"Nope. Just five hundred bucks. Up front. That's all it takes."

With that introduction, the contest began. One by one,

the "gals" bounded to the microphone and announced in an overmiked squeal: "Hah! Ah'm Tiffany!" "Hah! Ah'm Amber!" "Hah! Ah'm Heather!" And on through Tara, Toya, Darla, Audra, Monica, Ashley, Stacie, Kristi, Traci, Melanie, Kimberly, April, Danielle, Janelle, Jo-elle, Nicole, and thirteen others.

Some were cute, some pretty. Some even had that rarest of qualities in any teenager: poise. A contest official had told us that while some of the contestants were first-timers, others had participated in as many as a hundred shows before "graduating" (her word) to this pageant. Some had started as three-year-olds in the Miss Tot South Carolina contest, then worked their way up through the maze of contests sponsored by local chambers of commerce, rotary clubs, businesses, and schools. On the stage before us, in fact, were a former Miss Sweet Potato, a former Coon Dog Day Queen, and a reigning Miss Hub Cap.

The next morning was set aside for The Interview, which counted for 25 percent of each contestant's total score. The judges assembled in a hotel meeting room set with a row of tables, one for each judge. After breakfast (catered by McDonald's), a pageant official, a former winner herself, took pains to explain why, contrary to all expectations, *talking* was a part of the selection process. "The winner will have to officiate at many public events," she pointed out. For example: "The reigning Miss South Carolina recently appeared at a poultry contest and a brick-factory opening." That explanation satisfied Steve and me, but the two elder judges, the bald one in particular, still seemed put out by this "talking thing."

"Each interview lasts three minutes," the pageant official

continued. "At the end of three minutes, I will sound this bell, and the girls will move on to the next judge." She rang the bell. It had an appropriate game-show tinniness. "Now remember," she admonished us yet again, "this is not the Miss America contest. Don't ask the girls anything challenging."

"What kind of things should we ask?" inquired one of the decorative younger men.

"Well, don't ask about politics or religion." (There went my question about abortion!) "Don't ask them about the world situation, at least not in the political sense. Don't ask them about domestic problems. Again, that's too political. Of course, it goes without saying that you shouldn't ask anything about their . . . uh, *personal* lives — boyfriends, things like that."

I raised my hand. "What *can* we ask them about?"

"I was getting to that," she scolded. "You can ask them what classes they like in school and what they want to do when they get out of school. Those are perfectly safe."

The bell sounded and the next round began.

After listening to thirty-two girls who all wanted to be doctors or teachers and help save humanity — or at the very least work with underprivileged kids — I gave a perfect ten to the bosomy redhead who confided, "I want to go into business and make big bucks."

For the final stage of the contest, the evening gown competition, we reconvened at the local college. Steve and I and the other judges were directed to a long table down front, so close to the stage that the bright, unforgiving stage light spilled all over us — giving me a new surge of sympathy for the contestants.

Meanwhile, the auditorium behind us filled up with rest-less parents and families: mothers in thirty-dollar 'dos, little brothers gagged up in suits and ties, younger sisters with tissues stuffed in their bras, fathers with suspicion and anger in their eyes as they surveyed the panel of judges. When I accepted this mission, I thought the only real threat to my safety would come from a (rightfully) crazed Andrea Dworkin or Gloria Allred. Now, as I craned my neck to see the rows of suspicious eyes on me, I felt murder in the air from every direction.

But we were trapped. We had to choose.

As Steve and I and the other judges tiptoed out of the au-ditorium later that night, after the winner had been crowned and taken her victory promenade, a man in the au-dience, obviously the father of a losing contestant, ap-proached us. He was surrounded by his beautiful wife, two beautiful younger daughters, and two handsome sons, but he had anguish on his face and tears in his eyes. He wanted to know what, oh what, could his daughter do to improve her chances the next time around?

None of us had the heart to tell him. His beautiful, articu-late, and poised young daughter never had a chance. At five foot three, she just didn't have the legs.

The morning after our return from the pageant Steve and I met with our banker, Sharon Bellingham — the real owner of Joye Cottage. Sharon was a strikingly beautiful woman in her thirties, with jet-black hair, skin like a bisque doll, and the kind of perfectly sculpted, upturned nose that you would expect to find on, well, Miss America.

Naturally, our recent adventures in Myrtle Beach prompted Steve to wonder aloud if Sharon had ever participated in a beauty pageant. Indeed, she looked like a natural. Had she been on the stage the night before, she would have gotten both our votes.

Sharon didn't even look up from our financial statements. "Why on earth would I want to do that?" she said, crinkling up her perfectly sculpted nose.

Back at the house, Mordia was in a funk. He had seen a picture of the winner on TV. She was white. One of the runners-up was black. "You know, the sister should have won," he said under his breath as I passed.

Still, not even Mordia's distress could tarnish our title of beauty pageant judges. Months later, when it was announced that our biography of Pollock had won the Pulitzer Prize, there wasn't anything like the same electricity in the air. We took the prize money and bought a tractor-mower with it, a good one, a John Deere. Thereafter, the crew referred to it as "the Pulitzer" — as in, "the front yard looks a little ragged. Better fire up the Pulitzer."

29.

Scandal in the Sewer

Celebrity, of course — even small-pond celebrity — has its price. Late one winter day, after the workers had all left, I heard a knock at the door. Knocks were unusual at any time because the door to the wing where we were encamped was far removed from the driveway and the street. With so many other doors and porches between here and there, most people gave up the search for inhabitants long before they found us. Which suited us just fine — except when we tried to have pizza delivered.

But this was definitely not pizza.

Standing in the doorway were two men. Both looked to

be in their fifties, and both were similarly costumed: steel-toed cowboy boots, pearl-buttoned cowboy shirts with tufts of dark hair showing at the neck and forearm, wide studded leather belts with big silver buckles, and cowboy hats — one black, one straw. Something strange was stuck on the front of the straw one, like a hood ornament. On closer inspection, it proved to be the head of a snake, its mouth open, fangs showing, as if ready to strike out from the hat of this lopey stranger. But there was something in his mouth — the snake's, that is. An American flag. Somebody, either this cowboy or his haberdasher, had put a tiny American-flag lapel pin in the snake's mouth, so it appeared to be either swallowing or spitting up Old Glory. Looking at the wearer, I decided this was a patriotic statement.

I consider myself as patriotic as the next man, so I framed my greeting cordially. "Can I help you?"

The man with the snake head looked at his partner and licked his lips nervously. "Well, yessir," he began in an accent so molasses-thick it almost had to be a put-on for the tourist trade, like the costumes at Williamsburg. "Is thissere where them two people live?"

"Which two people would that be?"

"You know," he clarified, "them two fellas what won the Nobel Peace Price?"

I liked the sound of that. "Pulitzer," I corrected.

"Well, Mr. Pulitzer, are you one of them fellas? Somebody said we should come to you 'cause we got this book that needs to get wrote."

Oh, no, I thought, not that. Not a book that needs to get wrote. When you're a writer, everyone who ever thought about writing a book thinks you are just the person to help them get it published or, better yet, write it for them. "I've got this great story," they always say. "I just need someone to write it down." As if the only thing that stands between them and *Madame Bovary* is a typist.

And just what was this great story that the man with a snake head on his head needed someone to write for him?

"It's about the Amelia sewer scandal." And then, defensively, "You ever heard of it?"

Of course we had. We had been watching the high drama unfold in the local headlines for almost two months. It seemed that the small town of Amelia, not far from Aiken, had decided some years back to build a new sewage plant. But instead of just buying a plot of ground to build on — land, after all, being cheap and plentiful in this rural area — the local politicians decided to build on *rented* land instead. The savings would be enormous, they claimed, because the owners of the land would charge the city only $5 a year in rent. What a deal.

Except for one thing. That $5 rental fee applied only to the *first year.* After that, the rent went up like a bottle rocket: $1,000 for the second year, $5,000 for the third year, $10,000 for the third year, etc., etc., until eventually it hit the astronomical sum of $200,000 a year — I don't remember the actual numbers, but you get the idea — far more than the land would have cost to buy outright, and far, *far* more than the citizens of tiny, one-stoplight Amelia could afford to pay.

Unfortunately, the fine print of this rental agreement didn't come to light until after the plant had been built and the town was already alarmingly deep in debt. After months of investigation, the banks that had financed the project and the state officials who were supposed to supervise it discovered what everybody in Amelia already knew: Town officials had been in cahoots with the owners of the land. They all got rich. Big deal. It was a story as old as small-town politics. Hadn't anybody seen *Chinatown?*

But our two visitors had a different precedent in mind. "It's the biggest story to come out of these parts since *Gone with the Wind*," said the one who wasn't wearing a snake head.

"Perhaps that's true," I lied. "But I don't think a New York publisher would be interested." Everyone *knows* how provincial New Yorkers are.

The two men wouldn't take no for an answer. "The story's so complex," they chorused. "There's so much involved. So many people going to jail. It's like an octopus with all these different tentacles reaching out all over the place."

This story was like an animal, all right, but one with paws, not tentacles. "I don't think so" was all I said.

"We got all kinds of inside information," they protested. "We got access to all these here documents."

"I don't think so."

"But the mayor's mixed up in it! It's as big as Watergate!"

"Trust me," I finally said. "If the *governor* were involved. If he killed fourteen people, chopped their bodies into little pieces, and stuffed them in the sewer, I still don't think it would make a book."

That, of course, wasn't true, but it stopped them in their tracks. "B-b-but . . . ," they stammered.

"In fact," I continued, "I can't remember a worse idea for a book."

Actually, that wasn't true either. Steve and I had been responsible for some worse ones ourselves (e.g., *The Harvard Business School Guide to Sex and Romance*). But it did the job. With a look of deep distrust — was I, too, part of the cover-up? — they shuffled back to their pickup truck. I wanted to suggest that they take their story to Oliver Stone or, better yet, go into the hat business, but decided I had done enough damage to the reputation of the Nobel Peace Price for one day.

30.

The Weeping Room

Ever since our arrival, we had been meaning to pay a call on Meta Bainbridge, a woman who used to work for the Whitneys, but several months passed before we dared leave the work site unsupervised.

She lived not far away on a rough clay road that skirted Hitchcock Woods — a twelve-hundred-acre tract of woodlands donated to the city by, among others, W. C. Whitney. Aiken city fathers liked to refer to the woods proudly as "the largest urban park in America," which was technically true, I guess, because it lay mostly within the city limits. But Central Park it wasn't. Rough, confusing trails and dense underbrush were enough to turn a Sunday stroll into a survival test. Much too much like the real outdoors.

Meta's house belonged to a row of small cottages (*actual* cottages, in this case) that were built at the edge of the woods near the big houses like Joye Cottage to quarter black trainers and stablehands back in the days when everyone who had horses had servants to take care of them. Aiken's first black church, we were told, was built down there in the lap of the forest, hard by Coker Spring, the water source that had first attracted settlers to the area in the early 1800s. For the rest of that century, black women congregated at the spring to do the town's wash. Between the coming of municipal water and the breaking up of the big households, however, most of the blacks had left the area. The church was long gone, although if you hacked through the weeds, you could still see the stone base where the baptismal font once stood.

"I was baptized in that church," Meta said, pointing from her porch as if she could see it. As if she could see.

Meta, who was blind, shared her little frame house with another woman, Louise Meadows, who cooked and cleaned and kept her company. But the house itself had long since passed out of either woman's control. Mushrooms grew from the sodden wood under the eaves, and tall weeds sprouted around the tires of an ancient Corvair in the back-yard. A rug hung over the porch rail as if to dry, but you could tell by the fading on one side that it hadn't been moved in months, maybe years.

The front room was tidy, but cluttered — as if nothing had ever been thrown away, just dusted and straightened. In one corner, three television sets were stacked one on top of the other: the bottommost, the biggest, a ponderous wooden cabinet from the fifties with a tiny screen; on top of that, a less bulky, metal-clad model from the sixties; and on top of that, a small plastic set from the seventies, its fuzzy black-and-white image flickering in the dense air. The furniture around the walls looked as if it had been salvaged from decades of discards: a nubby green sofa here, a faded floral chintz chair there, doilies everywhere covering the worn spots. Nothing wasted, nothing lost.

Meta felt her way to the faded flowers of one chintz-covered chair. "My mama said that house has lots of secrets," she began.

"Your mother?"

"She worked for Miz Whitney, too."

"Which Mrs. Whitney?"

"Why, the first one, of course," she said. "Miz Edith." In fact, Meta's mother had started work at Joye Cottage in 1897, the very year W.C. rebuilt it for his new bride. How old was Meta at the time? "Six," she said, which made her ninety-eight.

"Mama died in 'sixty-seven," said Meta. "She was a hundred and two. That's her there." She pointed the crooked branch of a finger at a sepia picture on the wall showing a light-skinned black woman in long skirt and apron standing next to a white woman in silk derby and cutaways.

I started to figure. "So your mother was born —"

"No sir," Meta interrupted my calculations, "my mama was born a free person — *after* the war." She, too, meant the Civil War.

"Can you tell us anything about Mrs. Whitney?" Steve asked.

Meta looked surprised. "You hasn't seen the ghost?"

The ghost?

"Miz Whitney's ghost!"

We had heard vague, half-joking talk about Joye Cottage being haunted, but dismissed it as typical small-town Boo Radley stuff. Now our ghost had a name, and that changed everything.

"Mama said she come back to her room after she died," Meta explained, very matter-of-factly, as if explaining the comings and goings of a distant (but still-breathing) relative. "And she's still there."

Exactly which room was that? we wondered.

Meta closed her eyes, tilted her head back, and guided us through the house without a misstep. Starting in the kitchen, of course, not the front hall, she talked us through the staff dining room, the pantry, the main dining room, the billiard room, the salon, and the back hall, describing long-vanished furniture as she went. Finally, we arrived in Miz Whitney's chamber, a vast room with a big bay window at the far end of the house that we had designated the master guest room.

"This is it," Meta announced, seeing the room clearly in her mind's eye. "The Weeping Room."

The room I saw in *my* mind's eye certainly made *me* want to cry. It was the same room I had seen in real life only a few hours earlier, when Steve and I joined Eugene the plasterer to assess the devastation. No room in the house needed more work. On every wall, great brown water stains streaked the old floral wallpaper almost to the floor, and the plaster bulged everywhere. In places, it had broken through and fallen away in gruesome chunks, leaving gaping, dusty wounds edged in shreds of cabbage roses.

We had asked Wilma Hazlett (too late, as usual) if she knew anything about the leaks or what might have caused them. She had said they were the remnants of a leaky skylight, long since closed up.

But Meta had a different explanation. "That skylight never leaked," she sniffed, when we told her about the sorry state of "Miz Whitney's" room and, we thought, the reason for it. "Those ain't water stains," she insisted. "Nossir. Those are *tear* stains. That's what Mama said. Miz Whitney loved that house and that house loved her. And when she died, it wept for her. *Wept*. That's why Mama called it the Weeping Room."

It was, we discovered, a fitting name for the room of a woman who, by all accounts, rarely knew happiness.

Everywhere Steve and I looked to learn more about our resident ghost, in history books and family accounts, we found a sad, frustrated woman: a bridesmaid to happiness, never a bride. As the eldest daughter of a blue-blood Boston physician living in Manhattan, she enjoyed a privileged upbringing. But New York society looked down on Brahmins — too stuffy and badly dressed, it was said. When Edith's sister Caroline was courted by a very rich and powerful man, James Gordon Bennett, owner of the *New York Herald* and the publicity genius who sent Stanley to look for Livingstone, New York society dismissed him as a "bouncer" — a social climber — fifteen years her senior and a drunkard to boot. Their courtship only embarrassed the family.

The Gilded Age was not an easy one for women — except, of course, brainless and wellborn women who would fare well in almost any era. But for a woman like Edith May — smart, curious, *and* wellborn, and looking for more out of life than a good table at Delmonico's and a first-circle box at the Metropolitan Opera — it was hell. The role that women were expected to play could be more confining and infuriating than an eighteen-inch corset on a twenty-six-inch waist.

A woman had to be "pure" — by which the Victorians meant not just stupid about sex, but serene and restrained in all things, uncontaminated by passion of any kind. But Edith *loved* riding. From the moment she learned to ride as a girl, she was mad about horses and everything having to do with them. In family photo albums, picture after picture shows her in pleated frock coat and derby, sitting astride a tall, breedy chestnut mare, hunting whip in hand, a most unladylike grin of enthusiasm on her wind-burned face. She was the white woman in silk derby and cutaways standing proudly, grinning still, in sepia immortality on Meta's wall.

A woman had to be helpless. No matter how decisive, capable, and competent she was in fact, she had to *appear* helpless, just as she had to appear clueless no matter how intelligent and well educated she was. When young Edith used her wits and stamina to survive a boat wreck in which several passengers drowned, her family didn't know whether to be relieved that she had come through or embarrassed by the stories of her bravery and resourcefulness in saving several of her friends.

A woman had to be dressed — not just dressed, *armored* — the more expensively, elaborately, and impractically the better. French clothes were best, especially in the most sumptuous fabrics — tulle over satin, spangled chiffon — laid over layers upon layers of undergarments, foaming, swirling skirts of embroidered lawn and lace flounces. And underneath it all, the steel truss of a corset, wound so tight around the middle that it tipped the wearer forward as she walked, according to one historian, "like the figurehead of a ship under full sail."

In fact, a woman's life in the Gilded Age was all about constraints, limits, "don'ts." Don't wait more than three days to call on a hostess after her dinner party. Don't take off your hat, veil, and gloves when making calls. Don't let a gentleman bow first — unless he's from Europe or the South. Don't introduce an older person to a younger person or a lady to a gentleman. Don't make calls with an unrelated male, even one to whom you're engaged. Don't use both hands to rearrange your skirt. When shaking hands, don't apply too much pressure or hold your hand too high. Don't be the first to wear a new fashion. Don't give out the name of your dressmaker.

Even in relaxation, there were rules. Women like Edith May who liked to ride had to do so sidesaddle, a dangerous and ungainly position — "like sitting on the running board of a speeding car," one woman called it — the sole advantage of which was that it allowed a woman to keep her legs together. Far from leaving the constricting bustles and corsets behind when they took to the open fields on horseback, women riders wore starched linen collars and cuffs and heavy woolen habits with tight, padded shoulders even on the hottest days. A few allowed themselves the illicit pleasure of pants, but only hidden under long woolen skirts. And no lady would ever be seen in public — on horseback or otherwise — without a hat and gloves.

Edith longed to break away from this iron etiquette. She bridled under the constraints on female activity as under the suffocating sumptuousness of her clothes. In secret, she learned to ride astride, with the strong back of a sturdy Thoroughbred *between her legs*.

So it wasn't any surprise that — at a time when Victorian mothers routinely told their daughters, "Don't marry for money, but marry where money is" — young Edith married for love. On a trip to Europe, a dashing English officer, a captain in the Queen's Own Hussars, swept her off her feet and then followed her back to America. After they married, he resigned his commission, fathered two children, then settled down to the quiet life of a pensioner living on his wife's money. Still in her midthirties, Edith found herself "retired" — trapped in a dull, loveless marriage to a lazy, leeching man.

When he died, only a few years later, she felt free again, but it was seven more years before she fell in love with another man. It happened on a trip to Aiken, South Carolina, to visit friends, and this time she followed her mother's advice: The man was W. C. Whitney.

There was a different problem this time, though. He was married.

Then, in 1893, W.C.'s wife Flora died, and Edith May had another close brush with happiness — perhaps her closest. After the proper period of mourning (during which the two continued to see each other), W. C. Whitney asked Edith May Randolph to marry him. There was one catch, however. He wanted to do it immediately — "the day after tomorrow," in fact — before family and friends could be informed, before they could express their outrage, before they could intervene. Instead of joyous and convivial, Edith's second wedding would be sudden, hurried, and summary — "like an execution," quipped one of the few witnesses.

As it turned out, W.C. was right to hurry. When they learned (after the fact) of their father's remarriage, his children were shocked and appalled. "Of course your marriage was a great surprise," wrote son Harry with chilly understatement. Oliver Payne, Flora's brother, called the marriage "treachery" against his dead sister, and set in motion the awful machinery of avarice that would tear the Whitney family apart and break W.C.'s heart.

And for all this, of course, Edith blamed herself. So much sadness in so short a life.

Desperate to escape the frustration and sadness and guilt, determined to restart her life with W.C. without the meddlesome, disapproving world looking on, Edith sought a new place to call home, a place far from New York and

Long Island and Bar Harbor and Newport and all the gilded ghettos of "people we know." She knew she could never settle into W.C.'s huge Fifth Avenue palace; that was and always would be Flora's house.

So Edith escaped to the place she loved most, the out-of-the-way place where she could live outdoors, in the clean air, on horseback; the place where she could wear pants and ride astride and not cause a scandal of snickering; the place where she had met and, some said, first made love to W. C. Whitney.

She escaped to Aiken.

A subversive act required a subversive house, and that's exactly what Edith Whitney built — or, more accurately, what W.C. built for her — in the sandy pine barrens of the Savannah River. The houses of New York society were great stone castles built in styles that spoke in stentorian tones of power and privilege: Empire, Romanesque, Queen Anne, Renaissance. There was a Cheopsian ambition about all of them, a hyperventilating insistence, in stone and mortar, on the rightness and permanence of wealth.

Of course, almost all of them are gone now.

Even when they moved to the country, the elite brought with them their delusions of grandeur, surrounding their huge country houses with guarded gatehouses, castellated towers, and palatial outbuildings. If Edith had been a Vanderbilt, she could have moved to Aiken, or anywhere for that matter, and built a Biltmore, the immense stone château that George Vanderbilt imposed on the bucolic little town of Asheville, North Carolina.

But instead, she chose Joye Cottage.

Instead of erecting a brand-new stone manse that

pretended to be old, she renovated a rambling country inn that truly was old (by American standards, anyway). Instead of filling it with the usual Victorian clutter — bibelots, tapestries, and fringed mantelpieces; embroidered pillows, footstools, and ottomans; polar-bear rugs, ruffled lampshades, and linen doilies — she sent a shopping list of necessities to Grand Rapids (a bed and dresser for every bedroom) and left the rest restfully bare. Instead of creating the usual dim, chapellike interiors — heavy, tassled curtains, gilded lambrequins, portieres over the doorways, and woodwork and wallpaper in dark hues of chocolate, burgundy, and olive (the favorites in New York) — she painted the wood in shades of white and cream, hung the beds with muslin and the windows with sheers that let in the clear Carolina light, and papered the walls in bright floral prints, especially her favorite, cabbage roses.

In short, she threw off everything New York, just as she had thrown off the tulle, satin, chiffon, and lace and broken free from the straitjacket of corsets and calling. For Edith, Aiken wasn't just a relatively obscure resort where her husband and a handful of rich friends liked to hunt and shoot and play the newly fashionable games of polo and golf, it was a place where she could, at last, be herself. And Joye Cottage wasn't just a house in the country; it was the first place she had ever felt at home.

So W.C.'s great Christmas party for the opening of Joye Cottage in 1897 was both a homecoming for Edith and a wedding celebration. The two lovebirds had been married less than three months, and already friends were noting a remarkable change in the groom. They described him as "supremely happy." With a radiant Edith at his side, he seemed to enjoy life more, and enjoy his power to make others enjoy — which was considerable. "He had entered his true metier," a biographer wrote, "as the host who delighted in treating his guests to every luxury of food and entertainment regardless of cost, yet was so evidently pleased about it that he seemed to do it out of hospitality rather than ostentation."

And then, suddenly, it was over.

On a beautiful winter day, after the big party and after a magnificent Christmas in Joye Cottage, the newlyweds joined a group of friends on a hunt through the vast woodlands around Aiken that W.C. had purchased with his friend Thomas Hitchcock Jr. The quarry that day was a deer the servants had captured and let loose for the occasion. Thundering in pursuit, the riders approached a low tree limb and, one by one, bent down to clear it. And if Edith had been riding her own horse that day, she too would have cleared it. But the horse she happened to be riding was two hands taller than her usual mount. And that made all the difference. Her head struck the limb at full gallop, her horse ran out from under her, and she dropped to the ground in a motionless heap.

When W.C. saw what had happened, he yanked his horse around so hard, it reared and stumbled and, if it hadn't been for extraordinary horsemanship and sheer will, would have fallen. Witnesses said later that they had never seen a horse reverse direction so quickly; that it looked like horse and rider had turned around in midair. Within seconds, W.C. was holding his wife's still body in his arms.

Back at Joye Cottage, a doctor who happened to be a houseguest treated the six-inch gash in Edith's head and determined that she had suffered severe damage to her spine. The diagnosis was no sooner out of the guest's mouth than W.C. contacted two of the best doctors in America, Charles L. Dana and C. F. Bull, and ordered a special train to bring them from New York at breakneck speed. "TAKE SPECIAL TRAIN," he wired them frantically, "AND DON'T LOSE A MOMENT."

Less than thirteen hours later — a stunning time for a journey that usually took days — the two doctors arrived in Aiken. They told W.C. that Edith had a broken cervical vertebra and put her in a plaster cast from head to hip.

It was three days before she regained consciousness. And when she did, the first thing she saw, sitting among the cabbage roses of her bedroom, was W.C. He had been there the whole time, taking his meals on a tray and refusing any sleep except at her side. He stayed there for the next two months, ignoring his businesses, old friends, even his horses, until the doctors decided Edith could safely return to New York.

W.C. took personal charge of the trip. He hired a special train of four Wagner Palace cars and personally helped lift Edith, ever so gently, through the window of the coach because her cast wouldn't fit through the door. When they arrived in New York, he helped move her from the train to the boat that would take them to his Long Island estate, and then from the boat to the specially adapted carriage. He made sure all the streets were closed to traffic on the last stretch of road so the carriage would not have to stop. He even walked alongside the carriage as it made its slow, arduous way, keeping one loving eye on Edith to detect the slightest wince of discomfort and the other anxious eye on the roadway. If he spotted any debris, no matter how small, that might cause the carriage to bump or jolt, he would rush ahead to pick it up. Mile after mile, thus he smoothed her way.

Nor did he stop when she was finally settled into the big shingle house in Old Westbury. He spent the next few months by her bedside, poring over medical texts searching for the miracle that had eluded the specialists. His daughter Dorothy remembered "passing the open door of Papa's room every evening and seeing him beside his desk reading all the medical books he could lay his hands on. He hoped always to find some answer to this cruel and implacable fate."

But implacable it was. More than a year after her fall, Edith Whitney died with the man she loved at her side, but far from the house she loved.

31.

Winter Colony

Did we ever encounter the ghost of Edith Whitney? No, but there was a moment when I thought we did. I was working in the house past dark one evening not long after being told of poor Edith's fate when I heard a sound on the veranda and looked up to see a face in the window, a woman's face.

It turned out to be our neighbor and the former mistress of Joye Cottage, Joan Tower. A highborn socialite whose aquiline, deco beauty had landed her twice on the cover of *Life* (it didn't hurt that her husband at the time was Elliot Elisofon, the famous *Life* photographer and *African Queen* cinematographer), Joan later married the last Whitney who lived in the house and, much to her dismay, was forced to sell it when the marriage ended in divorce. She had watched in pain as the house disintegrated under the neglect of Mr. Kane, and now had come to meet the new owners.

Although a far sleeker and more worldly woman than Edith Whitney, to go by the old photographs, Joan reminded me in many ways of the first First Lady of the house. Like her predecessor, she came from a different, gentler time. She told stories of riding in the backseat of her grandfather's cane-sided, open-fronted Renault town car, with the family's English chauffeur, Edwin, behind the wheel, and the family's stately Airedale, Chummy, in the seat beside him, its right paw draped over the door as lightly and elegantly as a lady's gloved hand. "It was the most beautiful car in New York," according to Joan, "and every policeman in the city knew that car and that dog." On holiday shopping trips down Fifth Avenue, her grandmother bought presents specially for every servant, Joan would recall proudly, because she knew and loved them all that well.

Also like Edith, Joan was the hub of social life in Aiken. Both while she lived in Joye Cottage and afterward, she gave the most elegant brunches, the most stylish parties, and the most spirited dances.

The Whitneys might have left, but the social structure they helped build lived on after them. Remnants of the baronial class that had followed W.C. and Edith to the edge of the known social world still lived in Aiken, although only a few still occupied the grand houses their ancestors built. And even for them, time had taken its toll. Heiresses born to balls and black-tie dinners and brigades of servants had seen their great households shrivel. As they grew up, their servants grew old and then began to die off. Where two maids, two gardeners, a cook, and a butler might have attended their christening, only a part-time maid was left to usher them into their dotage. For many, women and men, age eventually caught up with lifestyle, turning their parents' privileged indolence into little more than a colorful retirement: playing golf and riding in the woods by day, drinking and "calling" by night. Locals still referred to them as the Winter Colony although many were full-time residents now, and some even had children who had put down roots in the area — "going native" in a way unthinkable in W.C.'s day.

The fact that their former premier party venue had been bought by two writers from New York did not go unnoticed by the remnants of the Winter Colony. The news, announced in three-inch headlines on the front page of the *Aiken Standard*, was met in the town's most rarefied social circle with a combination of curiosity and alarm. The newcomers did not play polo, did not come from families with recognizable names, did not ride, did not collect sporting prints, and, most alarmingly, did not drink. And the one thing they assumed we did have in common — money — we didn't.

But that was only a faint hint of the gulf that separated us. Having lived for five years in Cambridge, Massachusetts, then ten more in Manhattan, where Republicans were as exotic as cannibals from Papua New Guinea, Steve and I suddenly found ourselves surrounded: two lone grains of Democratic salt in a sea of Republican mashed potatoes.

One night, after washing off the day's accretion of plaster

dust and frustration over the slow progress of work, we went to a dinner party at the home of one of the grandees of the Winter Colony. Normally, Steve and I tried assiduously to avoid such events, where we were inevitably expected to wear ties — a perversity of adulthood that we had successfully avoided for years. (People would ask me why, after graduating from law school, I never went into practice, and I would tell them unflinchingly, "It was the ties.")

The dinner was being held in honor of a group of visiting equestrians from Alaska, or someplace, and I was seated between the wife of an aging polo player with a *Fortune* 500 last name and a handsome, white-haired woman named Rosamond who said she was actually born and raised *in Aiken.*

"What are *you* doing here?" I asked.

She laughed. She had a charming, guileless laugh. "You know there *was* an Aiken before all *this,*" she said, embracing our fellow diners with a beatific gesture. She had the most strikingly blue-blue eyes — like the sky on a cloudless summer day — a crown of white-white hair, and an angular, dimpled face. Some women get softer as they get older; some get leaner. The same can be said of their minds: some sink into nostalgia and sentimentality; some discard everything inessential and arrive at a fierce sharpness. Rosamond was definitely among the latter.

"Aiken was one of the most beautiful small towns in the South once," she said. And I believed her. If Time had a voice, it would sound like Rosamond, with all the crackle and character of a worn old LP. Aiken was chartered in 1835, she told me, when a rich local landowner gave his daughter's hand in marriage to a railroad engineer in return for a promise that the railroad would put a stop and build a town on the landowner's plantation, called Chinaberry. ("No railroad for me," the landowner reportedly told his future son-in-law, "no girl for you.") In the end, everybody won: The daughter got her beau, the landowner got his stop, and the president of the railroad, William Aiken, got his name on the new town.

"We like to think of it as a wedding gift," said Rosamond with a twinkle in her sky-blue eye that said she recognized graft and civic corruption when she saw it, even in such charming, historical guise, and even from a distance of a hundred and fifty years.

Almost immediately, Aiken flourished. The new railroad line — the first passenger line in the entire country — brought wave after wave of visitors. First, it was wealthy Charlestonians escaping the steaming, malarial heat of low-country summers. Then, after the Civil War, it was wealthy Yankees escaping the bitter, interminable cold of northeastern winters. "This was about as far south as they could get," said Rosamond with another bemused smile. "The railroads didn't go to Florida yet." (The Civil War, that cruelest of wars, had been relatively kind to Aiken. Only one minor battle was fought in the area — within sight of the Joye Cottage — and that, a rare Confederate victory against Sherman's advancing troops. Best of all, the Union army had bypassed the town on its devastating march *back* from the sea toward nearby Columbia, which wasn't so lucky.)

To accommodate the flood of winter visitors, new hotels sprouted up all over little Aiken, from the vast, clapboard-sided Park in the Pines Hotel with rooms for five hundred guests to the smaller but tonier Highland Park Hotel. (Both hotels came down even faster than they went up, in spectacular fires.) When the hordes of winter-weary Yankees overwhelmed even these mammoth hostelries, the good citizens of Aiken came to the rescue, turning every spare outbuilding, every house with a spare room, every room with a spare bed into an "inn."

One of those who answered the call was Sarah Joye, a single woman from Charleston who owned an old farmhouse on the high ground overlooking the Sand River. For no reason in particular, other than its proximity to the woodlands where the richest Yankees liked to ride their horses, Miss Joye's cottage inn became the favorite of some of Aiken's poshest visitors, among them William Collins Whitney.

Rosamond's family had come to Aiken in 1843, she told me, not long after that famous "sweetheart" deal gave the town its start. They had already been here for generations when the folks from up north like W. C. Whitney discovered the place and "colonized" it in the name of New York society. For most of the one hundred years since then, her family and the dozen other old and prominent Aiken families had done business with the Winter Colony, but little else. (Amazing: Two tiny little spheres of elitism spinning side by side in a tiny little town, without touching.) It was only the common cause of historic preservation that had finally brought these two spheres into contact, landing Rosamond here in the parlors of the Winter Colony.

She described how Aiken had been transformed — actually, *devastated* was the word she used — by the arrival of the big bomb plant in the fifties. "We were victims of our own success," she said. And what a success it was. Thanks to the efforts of a few powerful southern senators, the federal government had poured almost a trillion dollars into the Aiken area at a time when other small southern towns were dying on the kudzu vine. At the time, the bomb plant was the largest single construction project *in human history,* even more mammoth than Hoover Dam. If all the materials used to build it had been loaded onto railcars, the resulting train would have stretched from the little depot in Aiken all the way back to Penn Station in New York.

Meanwhile, of course, dozens of big old houses were converted to SROs to accommodate the swarms of workmen that descended — or just bulldozed into oblivion to make way for the businesses that would cater to twenty-five thousand new, well-paid federal workers. Plantations were diced into tiny plots for housing developments; estates were broken up and sold off, plot by plot, until small tract houses filled the old rose gardens and parterres, and fences turned rolling lawns into checkerboards of rubber pools and barbecue patios. Instead of sitting at the ends of long, tree-lined vistas or luxuriating in acres of emerald lawns, the grand old mansions found themselves boxed in on every side by cookie-cutter houses sheathed in brick veneer and aluminum siding, like pieces of fine china packed in Styrofoam peanuts.

A town that had been narrowly spared by a civil war was nearly spoiled by a cold one.

The philosophy was simple: New is better. And it applied to trees as well as to houses. All up and down Laurens Street, towering old pines and huge, baroque elms were cut down to make way for power lines and light poles and, of course, parking. The town that horses built, the automobile unbuilt. Medians planted with hundred-year-old camellias and azaleas were simply scooped up and paved over to make room for more lanes of traffic or, of course, parking. It was somehow fitting that Chinaberry, the home of the grower whose daughter had started it all, and the oldest house in Aiken, was used as a boardinghouse for temporary workers at the bomb plant until its owner decided to trade the vast structure, including all the exquisite antiques within, for a '56 Oldsmobile.

But nothing compared to the day they tried to chop down the trees on South Boundary.

Early in Aiken's history, some conscientious, farsighted citizens had planted hundreds of live oak trees along both sides of the broad boulevard that marked the southern boundary of the town — South Boundary Road. In the century since, those little oaks had grown high and wide, their huge limbs intertwining over the street to form a majestic canopy almost a mile long. We had driven down South Boundary many times and still slowed whenever we entered that tunnel of dark arches, leafy vaulting, and dappled sunlight.

And they were going to chop all that down!?

With stunning calmness, but ice in her eyes, Rosamond explained how the electric company had strung its wires from poles that ran alongside these magnificent oaks, so that over time the tree branches and the electrical lines began to compete for the same space. The solution was obvious (to the electric company, anyway): The trees had to go. They couldn't let a few old trees stand in the way of progress.

"Did the town's elected officials stop them?" I asked. The trees, after all, were still standing.

Rosamond fixed me with a withering look, a look at once cynical and sympathetic. In fact, when the people who lived along South Boundary complained to the city about the power company's plans, the city fathers tried to argue that sweeping up the leaves that fell from that arboreal cathedral was costing the city *too much money*. So it was simply a matter of economics: The trees had to go.

"Can you *imagine?*" said Rosamond with a steely indignation that turned her ice-blue eyes as hard as diamonds.

Fortunately, once again, the good citizens of Aiken came to the rescue. The morning the power company trucks arrived to start the demolition, all up and down South Boundary men and women who hadn't climbed a tree in decades clambered up the canopy's vast latticework and hugged the ancient limbs. This was their answer to the powers-that-be: If the trees go, we go.

But then, just as Rosamond's story crested in triumph, out of the corner of my eye I saw our hostess pick up a small silver bell by her plate and shake it ever so lightly, making a tiny, crystalline ring.

Within seconds, I was no longer hearing about the depredations of insensitive bureaucrats or the courage of tree-loving citizens, but listening instead to the woman on my right, the polo wife from Juneau, or someplace, talking about the difficulty of finding good stable help. It wasn't until later that I learned what everyone else at the table apparently already knew: The bell was a signal to change partners. Time to start talking to the person seated on your *other* side. Every fifteen minutes for the rest of the dinner, the bell sounded and everyone at the table performed this little do-si-do of small talk.

Several rounds later, after the polo wife had refocused the laser of her intellect on the difficulty of finding good *kitchen* help, my attention was drawn to a conversation across the table. There, a banker from Anchorage, or someplace, with a face-lift, a fake tan, and hennaed plugs, was holding forth on the problem of inner-city blacks in America. "I'll tell you what we ought to do about *that*," he was saying to Joan Tower, who was bearing the misfortune of being seated next to him with surprising good humor and an extra martini. "I think we ought to give them all a *test* when they're young."

I saw his wife, at the far end of the table, cast a worried look our way. She was a former ballerina, we were told, retired from the stage yet still considerably younger than her husband — and still dancing attendance.

"You give 'em all a test," her partner was explaining, "then you put the top ten percent on a college track. Pay for their education, find 'em good jobs."

"And what about the others?" asked Joan, unsure if the time had yet come to be appalled, but certain that it was coming.

"You set up camps, work camps, somewhere out in the desert in the Southwest — Nevada, New Mexico, one of those places — and you put them all in these camps," he answered stoutly, "like a modern-day CCC." He paused for a moment, immensely pleased with his erudition, then added with a smile, "It would be just like the Depression."

Rosamond and I exchanged horrified glances. It sounded more like Dachau.

And we weren't the only ones who thought so. Looks of sullen discomfort circled the table as a black man in a white coat poured coffee and brought the hennaed plugs an after-dinner drink.

Fortunately, someone broke the awkward silence with a tap on a goblet and a startling announcement: The Vice President of the United States, Dan Quayle, was coming to Aiken.

Steve and I looked at each other with exactly the same thought: Frank the hairdresser, bored again, was setting us all up for another multicar crackup on the infobahn.

But we were wrong. This wasn't a repeat of the Madonna bubble. Dan Quayle was no Virgin. The Vice President was giving a speech in Columbia, it turned out, and someone in his Secret Service contingent who procured horses for him in Washington also knew someone in the Winter Colony, etc., etc. It was a perfect fit. The veep liked riding, golf, and Republicans; Aiken had riding, golf, and Republicans in abundance. It was better than inevitable; it was ordained.

At the dinner table that night, the news was received with electric excitement. The polo wife to my right squealed, "Dan Quayle is coming!" in my ear, then turned to the person on her right and squealed it again. "Dan Quayle is coming!" Madonna, shmadonna. Who cared about some slutty purveyor of soft-core musical porn when the true leader of the free world (*real* conservatives didn't trust George Bush — it was almost a litmus test) was coming to *our* town?

Then, as the realization dawned that she would be gone by the time the great man appeared, she glumly returned to what was obviously her favorite topic: the difficulty of finding good help.

32.

The Last Grandee

My trip to get keys copied had taught me one hard truth about life in a small town: Socializing begets socializing. The more invitations you accept, the more you get. Thus, when Steve and I reconnected after dinner that night, we discovered to our horror that we had accepted four new invitations *apiece*. Eight events — all of which would require ties, no doubt — all in the next two weeks. At this rate, we would never finish the house — or another book or even a Sunday crossword puzzle. The Winter Colony was fast becoming the Winter-Long Cocktail Party.

And the first event on our schedule was the very next day. "Someone's taking us for a ride," Steve announced.

A ride in what?

"A four-in-hand."

A what?

Steve shrugged his shoulders. "Just when the man started to tell me, that damn bell rang."

So we had no idea what to expect the next day, at noon, as we waited — in coat and tie, of course — in front of the big front door of Joye Cottage.

It was a beautiful, late-fall day. The dogwood leaves had turned a rusty red but still clung to their branches despite the coaxing of a November breeze. The sky was a cold, cloudless blue — the cerulean of Rosamond's eyes — the sun warmed our faces against the chill, and a serene, Sunday quiet made us realize yet again how little we missed New York.

Just then, we heard a strange clattering sound in the distance. By the time the sound reached the end of our clay street, we recognized it. We had heard it in a hundred old westerns: the pounding of many hooves on dirt, the slap of leather, the creak of wood, the rattle of brass. The stagecoach was coming.

Only what appeared from behind the hedge at the entrance to our driveway was not like any stagecoach I had ever seen — on the silver screen or anywhere else. First came four magnificent matched gray-white horses, harnessed and blinkered in gleaming patent leather, their heads held high, their chests thrust forward, their sinewy, high-stepping legs pounding the clay in a restless chorus line, their sixteen hooves shaking the ground with a sound like distant thunder. Behind them came a huge, gleaming, black-and-red coach, as tall as a house, it seemed, glistening like a Chinese lacquerware box in the gilding of the autumn sun.

On the very top of the box, holding a maypole of reins, sat a stately, white-haired man in a tweed suit.

Jack Seabrook, we later learned, was pretty much all that was left of that great seasonal migration of the monied class — like a flock of rare, gorgeous birds — that had created winter and summer colonies in a succession of fashionable nesting grounds all up and down the eastern United States: from Bar Harbor, Newport, and the Adirondacks, to Sea Island, Palm Beach, and the Hamptons. To Aiken. Jack had houses in Vermont and New Jersey as well as Aiken (in addition to apartments in New York and London) and moved among them, according to the seasons, with a company of grooms and butlers and cooks, not to mention a dozen gray-white horses, several carriages, and a coach the size of a house. He had first come to Aiken twenty-five years before as the guest of another Winter Colony resident, a du Pont heiress, and liked it so much he decided to buy a place of his own. He loved good food and wine (especially champagne), dressed like the Duke of Windsor (a personal friend long ago), and drove a coach like Ben Hur drove a chariot.

It sounded familiar: multiple houses, horses, food, wine, friends, and frolic. Were we meeting W. C. Whitney?

Jack laughed at the comparison. "Anyone who drove a coach and four like Ben Hur would be dead very quickly," he said. "Not to mention the damage he would do to the passengers." He added that W. C. Whitney, in fact, probably never drove a coach and four at all. More likely he tooled around smartly driving a more chariotlike pair. How did he know? "I don't ever recall seeing Whitney's name among the members of the New York Coaching Club," he said. Jack, we learned later, was the club's president.

Also unlike W.C., Jack Seabrook made his fortune legitimately — and, even more amazingly, did it in an era of taxes, the SEC, and morality. In fact, he made it *twice*, the first time by working in the family agribusiness, Seabrook Farms, known in the 1950s as the world's largest vegetable grower. But that fortune was for his father, who later disinherited his three sons and sold the business. So Jack started over at the age of forty-two and made an even bigger fortune heading a worldwide conglomerate of shipping, utilities, trucking, and even Hawaiian sugar. No robber baron here.

As I climbed up into the seat beside him, I saw not W.C.'s angular features and prowling eyes, but a strapping, big man of strong Saxon good looks, with a big laugh and a full, groomed mane of white hair. He was wearing a flawlessly tailored glen plaid suit with a vivid red-and-yellow-striped bow tie.

"You look like a million bucks," I said without thinking.

He laughed lustily. "This is nothing," he said. "People who drove coaches *used* to wear morning clothes." That was in the glory days of the sport, Jack explained, before World War I and the death of Alfred Gwynne Vanderbilt, coaching's most glamorous popularizer, who went down with the *Lusitania* in 1915. (Jack was an astonishing fount of knowledge, both weighty and ephemeral, and it wasn't just his degree in chemical engineering from Princeton. Those closest to him said it was the result of a lonely childhood on the farm reading encyclopedias, two complete sets, from A to Z.)

I learned later that Jack himself had been instrumental in "dressing down" his sport, if you can call it that, to the point where tweed suits were deemed acceptable. But hats were still de rigueur for anyone riding on top of the coach, as we were. (Hats? And I thought neckties were a deal breaker.) Jack himself wore a gray top hat with a black band; his grooms, black bowlers.

"Walk on," he called to the horses in the calm but insistent tone of a grade-school teacher. And with what looked like only slight release of tension on the long leather lines in his hand, the whole great, jangling, creaking, slapping procession on which we were sitting began to move forward.

That procession had a name: the *Nimrod*. Built in London around the turn of the century — just about the time W.C. rebuilt Joye Cottage — it had somehow found its way to California, which was where Jack discovered it, forlorn and forgotten in a barn. While eating lunch in a diner on his way through the town of Tulare in 120-degree heat, he had overheard a conversation about a rancher with a "funny wagon" in his barn with the names of English towns lettered on its sides. What he found was a coach body, split and blistered by years of dry heat and neglect, and wheels reduced to a heap of sticks. After a restoration job worthy of an Old Master painting, including a repainting of the decorative panels by Aaron Shickler, portraitist to the elite, the *Nimrod* was reborn. Like Joye Cottage, only on wheels.

As I watched Jack maneuver this huge coach — weighing twenty-five hundred pounds empty, with room for fourteen passengers *on top* — with what seemed like the most casual of efforts, I wondered where he had learned such an ancient skill.

"From a book," he said.

Back in the sixties, apparently, when he was already a mature man, he had looked for a sport in which he could compete on more or less equal terms with younger men. That's when he decided to take up "driving" — as riding the reins on a coach, we learned, is properly called. Not that driving was easy. In fact, controlling and guiding four huge horses with reins held in one hand — thus the term "four-in-hand" — was not for the faint of heart or the weak of limb. Although he had ridden and driven horses since childhood — often driving customers around Seabrook Farms in a carriage and pair to show them the vegetables in the fields — the experts all said it couldn't be done. It was too late for him to learn, they said. Undaunted, Jack checked out a book about driving from the New York Racquet Club library and *taught himself* — a feat roughly equivalent to winning an Olympic figure-skating medal by taking a correspondence course.

I commented how beautiful the horses were, which elicited a proud smile. "They're Kladrubers," Jack informed me. "Czech. From a line developed in fifteen seventy-nine by Emperor Rudolf II for the sole use of the Viennese court and church." His stable also included some American Hanoverians, he said, and some Hungarian Lipizzaners (the snowy white horses featured at Vienna's famous Spanish Riding School): seventeen horses in all.

With a great burst of clattering as the horses' hooves moved from soft clay to hard pavement, we crossed Whiskey Road. Jack's coachman, Chris Higgins, a young man from Cheshire with a face straight out of Jane Austen, jumped from the back of the coach, positioned himself in the middle of the street, and raised a kid-gloved hand to stop oncoming traffic. Cars filled with Sunday tourists and families returning from church braked to a halt. Children pressed their faces to the windows, and adults craned their necks to watch as our grand, improbable, one-float parade clattered across the street.

"Chris is the best there is in this business," said Jack, pointing his whip at the incongruous figure of his bowler-hatted, tweed-suited coachman holding up a line of Aerostars, Suburbans, and four-by-fours on a two-lane road in a small, southern town.

We asked where Chris had learned his unusual trade.

"He used to work for the queen," said Jack.

Did he mean *the* queen?

He did. Elizabeth II. "Of course, the queen has many coaching teams," Jack noted. "But Chris served on the championship team, the one that Her Majesty sends to international coaching competitions. To lose there is to let down not just your owner but the entire British monarchy." How did Jack know all this? Simple. He knew the queen. He even stabled his horses at Windsor Castle's Royal Mews when he took them to England.

How, I asked, did he get six or eight of these huge horses to England?

"By Federal Express," came the reply.

We laughed incredulously. But Jack confirmed that it was true. Federal Express.

Did that mean he used FedEx to get his horses to Aiken,

too? (We knew how expensive it was to send a single letter overnight. How much for a *horse?* The mind reeled. Did they have a special box?)

No, Jack said with another big laugh. It was neither that simple nor that costly, though he did envy the ease with which horse owners of W.C.'s era moved their huge stables south every winter. "In those days, railroads were geared to transport horses in style," Jack explained. "Men like Whitney brought their horses on special railway express cars that were added to passenger trains as 'head end' cars, just behind the engine. The owners could come in luxury on the same train in their own private cars."

So how did Jack get his horses to Aiken? They traveled in an elegant Volvo horse van, complete with living quarters for the stable staff. The van held only six horses, so it took several round trips from his New Jersey farm for Chris to get the horses, carriages, harness, and livery to Nimrod South, as Jack called his Aiken place.

On the other side of Whiskey and back on clay, we rode past some of the remaining Winter Colony estates — some for sale, many in distress — like a gathering of faded *grandes dames* reliving the memory of some long-ago ball. We had driven these clay streets many times since coming to Aiken, but never like this. From our seats on top of the tall coach, we could see over the high brick walls that surrounded these hulking anachronisms. We could see from one house to the next, sometimes four or five houses at a time scattered among the hoopskirted magnolias and towering pines. What from street level seemed like a string of fortified plots, from atop *Nimrod* began to look, for the first time, like a neighborhood.

As we slowed to round a corner, a car in front of us pulled to the side of the road and a young boy, no more than eight years old, maybe less, jumped out. He stood motionless, mouth agape, watching us pass. The Kladrubers, as if sensing his gaze, put on their highest, proudest step as the great, glistening, red-and-black box rounded the corner. We were, indeed, a magnificent sight.

Just as we passed him, far below, he looked up at us with his big, wondering eyes and yelled, "Are you rich?"

"Nope," Jack answered, in a booming voice. "It's rented."

33.

A Great Baker!

It's hard to believe now, but in all our discussions of buying and renovating a sixty-room house, we never thought about how to keep it *clean*. Once, when we told a female friend in New York about our dream of owning Joye Cottage, she gave us a long, skeptical eye. "And which one of you is going to give up your career to dust?" she inquired.

In New York, an Ecuadoran woman named Rosa came in once a week, zoomed through our apartment in four hours, then was gone until the next week. And she left the place spotless.

Sometimes too spotless. We walked in one day and saw

that she had taken the paintings off the wall and was vacuuming them vigorously. (Why not? She vacuumed everything else.) Still, if she erred, it was in cleaning not wisely
but too well. How many Rosas would it take to keep Joye
Cottage clean? we wondered.

Searching through old W.C.'s account books, we found
our answer. Eighteen.

Eighteen? Steve and I looked at each other in utter disbelief, then despondency. What did eighteen people *do?* The
account books explained: five cooks, three housemaids, two
laundresses, two chauffeurs, two lady's maids, a valet, a
butler, a stoker, and a polisher. The stoker's job was to stoke
fires, we discovered; the polisher's, pretty obviously, to polish silver and brass. That was all they did, stoke fires and
polish brass, eight or ten hours a day, six, sometimes seven
days a week.

And that was just the staff that traveled with the Whitneys from New York (or, in some cases, preceded them, to
open the house). When they arrived in Aiken, those eighteen joined a permanent staff of five already in place, made
up mostly of local blacks like Meta and her mother.

And whenever a prominent guest joined the Whitneys in
Aiken (a redundancy; all their guests were prominent), the
staff grew even larger. The guests would bring their own
servants: usually a valet, a lady's maid, and, if they came by
car, a driver. Even members of the Whitney family brought
their own entourages.

And none of these figures included the stable help, which
could run to a dozen or even more if guests brought along
coachmen and grooms. They weren't considered part of the
house staff, however, because they slept in quarters above

the stable and ate food prepared by a special cook in yet another outbuilding.

In other words, when the house was crowded with guests (as it was that first Christmas), and every guest brought servants *and* horses, the Whitneys could have had *fifty people* running around Joye Cottage, keeping the place clean and neat and functioning smoothly.

We had Mrs. Johnson.

The only thing we knew about Mrs. Johnson when we hired her was that she was a *great* baker. We inherited her from a newly made friend, a thirtysomething stockbroker named Sam Stanford, who had also recently moved to Aiken — in his case from Tennessee, for a wife, not a house. Unlike us, however, Sam had brought his housekeeper with him, installing her and her invalid war-veteran husband in a double-wide trailer that he bought for them.

The trouble started almost immediately. Back in Tennessee, Mrs. Johnson had enjoyed full control of Sam Stanford's life and didn't take kindly to sharing it with anyone else, especially another woman, even if that woman happened to be Sam's new wife. Unfortunately for Mrs. Johnson, the wife in question was Margo Ullman, a former Paris model and Hollywood stunt rider. In her short, colorful life, Margo had been wooed by European noblemen and Hollywood luminaries — and brought them all to heel — before settling down to a quiet country life in Aiken, raising exotic birds and breaking eight-hundred-pound horses.

Soon after Mrs. Johnson's arrival, Margo informed Sam that her house wasn't big enough for both of them.

Thus Sam's generous offer of Mrs. Johnson's services to us, along with the single advertisement: "She's a *great* baker."

In retrospect, we should have known something was wrong as soon as she walked into the interview. Instead of a jolly, round woman with pink cheeks and flour in her hair, what stood before us was a ninety-pound stick figure of a woman, sixty years old, with tightly curled and exhaustively bleached hair. She eyed us with a deep and sour suspicion. Whenever we said anything that displeased her ("We don't allow smoking in the house"), she would close her eyes to razor slits and retreat into surly silence. Was this the vaunted baker? How could she eat her own sugary creations and stay so pencil-thin? And so sour?

And just when we thought we were imagining things, that she couldn't be as bad as that, she told us, in a hard-scrabble voice that came out of one side of her mouth, about the half dozen of her relatives who had been murdered back in Tennessee, mostly by other relatives. (Mrs. Johnson's accent, a product of deepest, darkest Tennessee, was absolutely impenetrable. Understanding it was not unlike watching one of those murkily miked, ponderously accented British films of the forties. You had to clear your mind of all distractions and stare intently at her lips. The rest was extrapolation: Considering the question, the context, and the expression on her face, what was she *probably* saying?)

Still. She was a *great* baker.

We had, of course, asked Sam's wife, Margo, for a recommendation. An extremely smart and extraordinarily blunt-spoken woman, Margo wanted to get rid of Mrs. Johnson more than anything in the world. As far as we were con-

cerned, all Margo had to do was give her a good recommendation and she was hired. Just one good word. "Take her if you want" was the best she could do. "But don't blame me. She makes my skin crawl!"

Still, Steve and I couldn't get those other words out of our heads: "a *great* baker." All the problems and all the warnings were crowded out by visions of bread — loaves and loaves of it, hot and fresh from the oven: multigrain, sourdough, zucchini, walnut, pumpkin, banana; pecan rolls split and grilled; cinnamon buns drizzled with icing; trays of soft, warm chocolate-chip cookies; chocolate, marble, and angel-food cakes; pecan, cherry, blueberry, coconut cream, and lemon meringue pies. Who *cared* if she couldn't clean? Who *cared* if you couldn't understand her? Who *cared* if she made your skin crawl? Bring on the desserts!

So strong was the pull of these confectionery visions that we didn't even stop to realize: We didn't have an oven. We didn't even have a *kitchen*, and probably wouldn't for another six months.

Still. Just knowing that a *great* baker was on the premises would make those months fly by. And in the meantime, we figured, surely her cleaning skills were sufficient to take care of three little rooms.

She did enjoy dusting. In fact, she enjoyed it so much that even with only three rooms to dust, she never seemed to finish dusting. No dust was safe from her. She was, indeed, dust's worst nightmare. The scourge of dust everywhere. The Anti-Dust. Wherever it tried to hide, she would hunt it down and wipe it out. Ruthless and implacable. In her daily quest for the perfect dust-free state, she displayed dazzling ingenuity. Every morning, she would find some cunning new battleground on which to wage her all-out war: baseboards, ceilings, walls, window blinds, tabletops, table *legs*, ceramic tiles, curtain rods, baseboards again, and, above all else, doors.

For a while it seemed that every time we returned to our three rooms during the day, Mrs. Johnson was dusting the doors again . . . still . . . working her dust rag in the tiniest of circles, millimeter by millimeter across the vast expanses of mahogany, with all the reverential care, excruciating patience, and glacial deliberateness of a Vatican conservator cleaning the Sistine Chapel ceiling with a Q-Tip.

Did I mention that we were paying her by the hour?

We asked Margo what could be wrong. How was this possible? How could Mrs. Johnson spend eight hours a day, five days a week, dusting three small rooms? If it really required all that, how would we ever keep the house clean when we opened the other fifty-seven rooms? If it required all that, W.C.'s roster of house servants would have read: five cooks, three housemaids, two laundresses, two chauffeurs, two lady's maids, a valet, a butler, a stoker, a polisher, and *twelve dusters*.

"Don't complain to me," said Margo with a dismissive toss of her head. "I warned you."

She had, indeed. But she couldn't resist explaining why Mrs. Johnson took so long to do so little: "When you aren't around, she isn't dusting, she's *sleeping!* She takes catnaps all day long." If we wanted to catch her at it, Margo advised, we had to surprise her. "If you're polite, and warn her that you're coming, she'll jump up and grab a rag. But if you tip-toe up the stairs, I guarantee she'll be sitting there with her head in her hands, out like a light."

Which is exactly how we found her the next day when we tiptoed up the stairs.

For five days we agonized over how to fire her — "You do it!" "No, you do it!" — but before we could decide who would do the dirty work, Mrs. Johnson did it for us. With-out warning (and without returning our keys), she high-tailed it back to Tennessee with her war-veteran husband, leaving us help-less once again and Sam Stanford with monthly payments on a used double-wide.

34.

Another Good Depression

Our experience with Mrs. Johnson left us more curious than ever about the "other side" of life in Joye Cottage: about the dozens of people (hundreds, over the years) who spent great chunks of their lives in our house, but were never mentioned in the history books, newspaper articles, or family letters. Unlike the Whitneys and their famous guests, whose lives were so amply and colorfully chronicled, the servants of Joye Cottage just seemed to have vanished.

All we knew about them was where they lived. In almost every wing of the house, tucked up under the eaves on the second floor, we saw their rooms: tiny, dim cells with low ceilings, dormer windows, no closets, and no fireplaces. In some areas, like over the kitchen, there were as many as eight such rooms, but never more than one bathroom to a floor. In some wings, there was no bathroom at all on the servants' floor, just a little sink in every room. They must have used chamber pots — or just waited till morning.

One other thing we noticed: There was not a single electrical outlet in any of the servants' quarters. At first we thought perhaps they were built before the house was electrified. But the downstairs bedrooms all had outlets. No, the reason was simpler than that. The Whitneys just assumed that their servants didn't need plugs because they didn't have anything to plug in.

What a shame, we thought, that we would never get a chance to speak with these faceless ghosts from the past. What stories they must have to tell.

Then one day we were recounting the story of Mrs. Johnson and her Anti-Dust jihad to our lawyer. "My wife's grandparents used to work at Joye Cottage," he said. Then, even more astoundingly: "They're still alive."

Three weeks later, on a drizzly November day, Howard and Eloise Latham returned to a home and workplace they hadn't seen in twenty years. They looked a little like ghosts: two pale, fragile figures in dark, funereal dress standing at the front door with their granddaughter. "They tried to go to the kitchen door," the granddaughter apologized as she introduced them. "I guess old habits die hard."

They stepped into the house as if sleepwalking, two sets of eyes scanning slowly back and forth across the workscape of sawhorses and uncut lumber. But the house

214 • ON A STREET CALLED EASY

they saw wasn't the gutted wreck we saw. The house they saw was inhabited.

"Mrs. Miller was very formal," said Eloise dreamily, without prompting. "She was from the old school. She was friendly, in her way, but there was always that wall."

We knew already that "Mrs. Miller" was Flora Whitney Miller, W.C.'s granddaughter by his first son, Harry — the son who stuck by him and his second wife, Edith; the son who refused Oliver Payne's Faustian offer and went on to marry Gertrude Vanderbilt; the good son who had inherited Joye Cottage and passed it along to his daughter. We knew that, despite the rift in her family, Flora Whitney had lived a fairy-tale childhood, from serving as flower girl at the marriage of her aunt Gladys Vanderbilt to Count László Széchényi, the last of the shamelessly extravagant society weddings of the Gilded Age (for which the count received $12 million), to being courted by a handsome young prince of the American aristocracy, Quentin Roosevelt, youngest of Teddy Roosevelt's four sons.

We also knew that Flora Whitney had seen her share of tragedy, starting when Quentin, by now her fiancé, was killed in World War I. He, like she, was only nineteen. (President Wilson, King George V, Clemenceau, and even the Germans sent condolences.) She went on to marry twice, bear four children, reign over New York society from her resplendent, art-filled apartment on Gracie Square, and shower the institution her mother founded, the Whitney Museum, with money, advice, and art. "She was a grand lady," Eloise summarized, then added enigmatically, "in her way."

"And she had grand friends, too," Howard supplied as he

drifted into the salon. "Did you know Fred Astaire used to dance in this room?" We didn't. We had heard about W.C.'s concerts with Caruso in the house, and Nellie Melba, of peach and toast fame, but not Fred Astaire. "He danced that wonderful tap routine from *Top Hat* just for us," said Howard as he spread his arms and did a slow, dreamy turn to the music in his head.

"It was a formal family, though," said Eloise in a scolding voice that brought her husband sharply face front.

Howard Latham, a short-legged terrier of a man who walked stiffly and always tilted slightly forward, his eyes fixed on the floor, tried to fill the ellipses in his wife's distracted commentary. He had spent so many years cleaning up after others, it seemed, he did it instinctively, even in conversation. "Mrs. Miller's children couldn't come to the house without being invited," he explained. "Even after they were grown up. They used to say to me, 'Why can't we be like other families and just drop in if we're driving through Aiken?'"

"*We* always came by rail . . . ," said Eloise out of the blue, as she gravitated through the dining room and toward the kitchen, leaving another fragment for her husband to tidy.

"Most of the staff came down separately," he obliged, "beforehand. But Eloise was house staff. She rode down on the train in Mrs. Miller's private compartment. She went everywhere with Mrs. Miller, even to Europe. I always drove one of the cars down. That was my job. The chauffeur was considered part of the stable staff, not the house staff." It sounded like an apology. "They had a big Lincoln, the kind with a Shelby seat in front."

"Shelby seat," Eloise sneered, coming out of her reverie

just long enough to humble her husband. "He means it had no roof over the chauffeur."

"Well, yeah, it did," Howard protested weakly. "When it rained, you had this canvas awning thing that you could put up there and these little supports —"

"But if the wind was blowing," Eloise interrupted, "you just got wet."

"Well," said Howard, making a last, nearly inaudible stand, "you had a cap to protect you."

They lingered in the kitchen for a long, long time. Howard pointed at the great black stove (which was scheduled for removal) and talked of waiting near its warmth for hours on cold mornings while the black cooks, local women, chattered and sweated. Eloise just looked and looked, until the sight of a roll of paper towels by the sink struck another spark of memory. "She didn't even know what paper towels were."

Howard explained. "One time, for some reason, the bills came to Mrs. Miller. Usually the butler paid them, but this time they came directly to her, and there was an entry for paper towels. She was reading this thing, and she said, 'Paper towels? What are paper towels?' She had never in her entire life heard of *paper* towels, and she was just horrified that such things existed."

Eloise smiled distantly. "I had great respect for her," she said.

"Should I tell them about Mrs. Miller and the porter?" Howard asked his wife.

"I don't think so," she cautioned.

But he told us anyway. "This was during the war, World War Two, and Mrs. Miller was traveling in her private compartment down here to Aiken with her dog, and the dog had a bed with silk sheets. And the porter, a colored man, he said to her, 'Do you know, madam, our boys are dying over there, and you have silk sheets for your dog!' He really told her. He did. But after that, it was no more silk sheets for that dog."

"I had great respect for her," Eloise repeated as a way of dismissing the story.

They wandered back through the house to a big corner bedroom that we were converting into a library. "This was Mrs. Miller's bedroom," Howard informed us as Eloise floated across the threshold ahead of him. The plaster was mostly gone, the walls mere studs, the chimney breast stripped to the brick, but Eloise saw none of these things as she slipped ever deeper into her reverie of remembrance. "Every day began with breakfast in bed," she said, looking to the demolished wall where the great Victorian bed had stood, "always in bed. I don't think she ever in her entire life had breakfast outside of her bed unless she was on a train."

Howard described how the kitchen maid would bring the breakfast tray to Mrs. Miller's door every morning, but it was Eloise's job to carry it from the door to the bed. "I had to be sure her pills were set right," said Eloise, who was following her husband's narrative even in the midst of her trance. "'Exactly two inches from the glass of water, dear. *Two inches.* No more, no less.'"

"If they were off," Howard continued, "even a little bit, Mrs. Miller would ring her bell, and Eloise would come running down the hall to move the pills."

"Sometimes no more than a centimeter," said Eloise.

Across the hall from Mrs. Miller's boudoir was a small

room (or a large closet, we weren't sure which) where we had piled old radiators and plumbing fixtures. Eloise peered inside for the longest time. "I spent most of my twenties and thirties in this room," she said, "and, come to think of it, my forties, too."

"Those women were all clotheshorses," Howard explained. "Sometimes Mrs. Miller would change clothes four times a day, what with swimming and lunch and bridge and dinner. That's a lot of clothes. Eloise spent most of her day getting the next outfit ready, pressing and folding and unfolding and pressing, and this was the room where she did it all. Whenever I needed her, this was the first place I looked."

Eloise got that distant look in her eyes again. "She thought we were fortunate just to be working for her," she said, more in nostalgia than irritation.

Howard supplied a story about a butler at Mrs. Miller's palatial home in New York who wanted to keep his own apartment. "'Well, why does he need an apartment?' she said. 'He lives *here*.'"

Finally, we followed Eloise upstairs to the little room under the eaves that had been her home in Joye Cottage for thirty years. She stared out the dirty dormer window for a long time. "From here, I could see your window," she said to Howard. "Over there." She pointed to another small window under the eaves of the old stable across the street.

"Mrs. Miller wasn't at all happy when Eloise and I married," Howard explained.

"It was a different time," Eloise hastened to add when she saw the look of surprise on my face. "Nobody's servants had families. Almost nobody married. They were afraid it would hinder your work if you had a husband or wife. Maybe you wouldn't want to work seven days a week."

"So I stayed over there in my room in the stables," said Howard, pointing out the window. "Eloise had to stay here."

Did people at least get paid well for such long, devoted, self-denying service?

"As far as Mrs. Miller was concerned," said Howard, "she put a roof over your head, and a meal on the table in front of you, and a uniform on your back. What possible use could you have for money?"

"She was very close with her money," Eloise added rue-fully, her soft, cabined voice — the result of a lifetime of "yes ma'am" and "no ma'am" and "in a minute, ma'am" — opening a window suddenly onto a vast landscape of resent-ment, then shutting it again just as quickly.

Howard could remember what happened when another chauffeur asked his employer for a raise. "She turned him down, of course. She said she could remember the days when servants made five dollars a week and were happy to get it because we were going through a Depression. 'What we need,' she said, 'is another good Depression.'"

35.

The House That Murphy Built

Four months into the project, with "Jingle Bell Rock" floating over the aisles of drill bits at the local builders' supply
and Christmas specials on nail guns at Lowe's, we were finally beginning to see some progress. J.T., the plumber, and
Dave, the electrician, working for considerably more than
five dollars a week, were busy replacing the old house's
sclerotic circulatory and nervous systems. Cutting through
the huge, rock-hard joists to run their wires and pipes, they
went through saw blades like Camille through Kleenex.
Bart, Manny, and the other carpenters (six in all) ran into
the same problem when they tried to drive nails with the

limp-wristed tap that had always worked for them in new construction. Over time, they developed a near reverence for the craftsmen who had put the house up a hundred years before without the benefit of a single Japanese power tool. But reverence or no, when the going got tough, they quickly resorted to nail guns, which just turned work into an indoor variation on their favorite outdoor recreation.

Still, amid the rubble and dust, through the whine of stalling saws and the report of nail guns, walls *were* going up. Eugene was working his magic on the old heart-pine bones of the place, and a few rooms were even ready for paint.

Or so we thought.

"You all ain't thinkin' of slapping any paint on them walls, are you?" asked Eugene one day when he saw us holding a book of color chips up against his freshly frosted wall.

Well, yes, as a matter of fact . . .

"You cain't paint new plaster," he laughed.

We found nothing funny about it.

"Plaster takes *months* to dry," Eugene explained. "If you slap a coat of paint over it, the water in the plaster will bubble up and lift the paint right off." I imagined sixty rooms, all molting at the same time. Not a pretty sight.

Why hadn't he told us this before — specifically, *before* he plastered most of the house?

"You didn't ask," said Eugene. "I thought you knew." In fact, we had asked him many times about the relative advantages and disadvantages of plaster. On more than one occasion, he had waxed expansive, even poetic on the former, but never uttered a discouraging word on the latter.

And he certainly never mentioned that plaster left you homeless. For how long?

"Oh, say, about six months," said Eugene.

"Six months!" We couldn't wait six months. We had been living out of suitcases for four months already. What did people do back in William Whitney's day, we wondered, when plaster was the only choice? Surely they didn't sit around for six months while their houses dried. W.C. and Edith moved into Joye Cottage only a few months after the groundbreaking! You can bet they didn't live with bubbly walls.

And neither would we.

Eventually, this bubble crisis, like all the others, passed. Over Eugene's harrumphing objections, we decided to use water-based acrylic paint instead of oil-based latex. That way, the moisture in the plaster could work its way through the paint rather than get trapped behind it.

And so it went, as we lurched from crisis to crisis, through all the possible permutations of "wrong" and "late" and "impossible": The lumber will be here tomorrow, they sent the wrong lumber, we can't get that kind of lumber. They cut the board too long, too short, too narrow, too wide. The room is too short, too long, too wide, too narrow. The light, the switch, the plug, the john, the sink, the drain, the tub *can't go there.* The windows are too big, send them back; too small, send them back; the wrong kind, send them back. The windows are late, late, late again. This isn't the faucet we ordered; this is the faucet we ordered, but it's broken; the faucet we ordered was shipped to San Francisco; they shipped the faucet we ordered, but the truckers are on strike; this is the faucet we ordered and they shipped it here and the truck delivered it unbroken, but the wrench slipped as we were installing it and . . .

Everything from kitchen appliances the size of Buicks to the most delicate of dentil moldings was subject to the iron law of Murphy. Slower than even the most cautious schedule, stronger than even the most paranoid safeguards, able to bust even the most Vanderbiltian budget in a single day, Murphy was our contractor, our crew, our buyer, and our accountant.

Murphy was the finish carpenter from up north who smoked marijuana on the job, or so we learned after the fact. He would light up a joint while cutting cornice and mellow out to the heavy metal whine of the miter saw. What better antidote to the nerve-jangling crack of the nail gun than a bongful of bliss? The crew called him Sick Nick. We thought they were just being funny. An unreconstructed hippie, Nick wore his wiry salt-and-pepper hair in a long ponytail, his jeans with holes, and his T-shirts tie-dyed. And he loved to talk. A simple "good morning" could unleash a full hour of chitchat, most of it about Nick's favorite subject, music. In fact, no matter what the question, the response was about music, which, for Nick, meant only one thing: "The Dead."

Because the house was so big and the opportunities to sneak a joint so many, Nick's stoning might have gone unnoticed for some time if he hadn't made one big mistake: He refused to use a level. Chemically transported into an altered and greatly exaggerated state of self-confidence, he believed that he didn't need tools, that his "eye" was enough. It wasn't. His first project — a small set of stairs — looked like something designed by Dr. Seuss.

Murphy was the beefy laborer named Lionel who soon distinguished himself as a demolition expert. A former army boxer with arms like legs and legs like torsos, Lionel considered every unwanted structural feature a personal affront, a sworn enemy to be obliterated by any and all means necessary. (According to Mordia, this was also the way he thought of his numerous girlfriends.)

We, however, couldn't help but be impressed by the violent precision with which he removed old plaster, stud walls, even concrete floors with nothing more than an ax, a sledgehammer, a crowbar, and a lot of anger. So when he asked us to buy him a high-tech electric saw called a Saws-All — to cut through nails, he said — we were surprised but agreeable. Just think how much havoc he could wreak with all that anger *and* technology.

We soon found out.

A few days later, J.T., the hunky plumber, emerged from the black hole of the basement with startling news: All the copper pipes were gone. One of the few workable systems we had inherited from the previous owners was an extensive network of copper pipes that carried water to bathrooms in the main part of the house. The biggest of these pipes was four inches in diameter, and the smallest ran for hundreds of yards in complex traffic patterns throughout the basement — a total of more than a fifth of a mile of copper veins, all in excellent condition. Now, all gone.

Lionel, it turned out, had broken in under cover of night

and systematically mined the mother lode of copper in our basement, which he could then sell for twenty cents a pound, the going rate on the black market — and a tiny fraction of what it would cost us to replace.

▲

But most of all, Murphy was the tile layer.

We had already gone through several tile layers by the time we got to this Murphy, whose name was Sam Foster. The others were probably all Murphys, too, but we never gave them a chance to prove it. The prices they quoted for the work we had to do were so inflated, we just assumed they were victims of the Joye Cottage Syndrome: a strange affliction that caused workmen to double or even triple their prices as soon as they drove up to our door. Over the phone, they would quote us one price — x dollars per hour or x dollars per square foot — for floor refinishing or landscaping or tile work. Then, when they saw the house, the price would mysteriously double or triple, bringing it more into line with the size of the house and, they mistakenly assumed, the size of our budget. It was the darnedest thing.

Sam Foster was the first tile setter we had found whose prices didn't seem subject to this strange malignancy. The price he quoted us for tiling the floor in one bathroom and fixing some broken tiles elsewhere, although a little high, remained steadfastly the same even after the full, sixty-room guided tour. A bald plug of a man with a pugilist's hands and nose, Sam even offered to seal the deal on the spot. That's how honest he was. We, of course, eagerly agreed and shook his meaty outstretched hand as a show of our good faith.

And desperation. In fact, by this time, the whole project seemed caught on the hook of undone tile work. Our several failed efforts to find a good tile setter had played havoc with the construction schedule. Until the tile was laid, the plumber couldn't install the fixtures; until the fixtures were installed, the painters couldn't paint the walls; until the walls were painted, the floors couldn't be refinished; until the floors were refinished, the carpenters couldn't lay the trim; and on and on. Like cars behind a braking engine, the work and the workmen were piling up behind this cow on the tracks.

Now, finally, Sam Foster was going to move that cow.

Except we didn't have any tile.

We had ordered a special tile from the West Coast — strangely, the only place we could find modern remakes that matched the old tiles used in the bathrooms of Joye Cottage. We had placed the order long before, but somehow the frantic search to find a suitable tile setter had obscured its status. Why fret about tile that we couldn't install even if we had it?

Now, of course, we had the tile setter but not the tile.

We called the manufacturer, screamed and yelled, slammed the phone down, and waited. And waited. Two days later, we called and screamed and yelled again. And then waited. And waited. Meanwhile, Sam Foster came to the house in the morning ready to go to work. He waited until noon for the delivery truck, disappeared for an hour, then returned with the rest of the workmen after lunch and waited some more. After a day or so of this expectant-father routine, Steve approached him. "You don't have to hang around here, Sam," he suggested gently. "We'll call you when the tile comes in." Sam smiled wanly — something he obviously did not do often — but refused to leave. He was getting divorced, he confessed, and "feelin' kinda lonely." Wouldn't it be all right if he just hung around the work site with a few of his friends on the crew until the tile arrived? What harm could there be in that?

What harm, indeed.

Eventually, the tile arrived — only it was the wrong tile. Apparently, some Murphy worked for the tile company, too. By the time we screamed and yelled some more and the right tile arrived by Express Mail, Sam Foster had been wandering around the house for two weeks, staring out windows, eating Little Debbie snack cakes, and making occasional conversation, but mostly just watching people work with a doleful, hound-dog expression.

Once the tile arrived, though, he worked like a trouper. In less than two days he was finished, and the logjam of jobs began to unjam. We were so grateful that we wanted to give Sam a bonus. Here, finally, was a workman who took his job seriously, bid honestly, worked conscientiously, and finished promptly. Our faith in the American work ethic was renewed.

And then he handed me the bill.

Two thousand dollars! For two days' work? I tried diplomacy: *"You must be crazy!"* I screamed.

"Listen," he said, immediately setting up defensive positions, "a hundred hours at twenty bucks an hour. That was our deal."

Twenty dollars an hour was, indeed, our deal, but *a hundred hours!* Ten would have been a stretch.

"I been here for two weeks," Sam grumbled as he

climbed into the cab of his pickup. "I kep' track of my time." Clearly, he was counting all those hours of "visiting" with friends on the work site, all those hours of waiting for the tile to arrive, all those hours of medicating the divorce blues with Little Debbie snack cakes and sports talk, all as *work!*

"That's ridiculous!" I screamed, ricocheting back and forth between anger and astonishment. "That wasn't work. It was *therapy!"*

"Are you callin' me a liar?" Sam snorted. He had clearly steeled himself for just this reaction and had his response ready. As he leaned out the window of his truck, the muscles in his neck tightened, his jaw pumped, and a lightning-bolt vein popped up on his forehead.

I'm sure I was undergoing a similar transformation. "Don't you play the school-yard bully with me," I said as I kicked some gravel at his tire.

He flung the door open and leapt from his truck. "And don't you give me any of your Yankee smart talk," he snarled (not knowing that I was a Yankee in accent only). "That's a fair bill and I expect to be paid."

I looked him in the eye but I could feel my knees getting rubbery. "I'll pay you what the work was worth," I said, "and not a penny more. Now get off my property."

He smiled. "Who's gonna make me?" He had a pugilist's smile, too.

For the first time, I felt the absurdity of the situation: this pathetic joint display of male dominance behavior. And I said so. "You've got to be kidding," I scoffed. "Does this approach work with your other employers?"

I could see he took my levity in the face of his threat as an insult. He stepped toward me. "You afraid to fight?"

"Oh, grow up," I said, and turned away.

As I did, I heard the sound of a foot making a quick take-off from the gravel behind me. He was coming at me. At almost the same instant, I saw Dave, the electrician, and J.T., the plumber, step out from behind Dave's truck. From the stern, fretful set of their faces, I could tell they had overheard the whole confrontation. I turned around just in time to see Sam freeze in his tracks no more than a foot from me. He, too, had seen Dave and J.T. and decided he no longer liked the odds.

"I think you better leave," J.T. told Sam, like the marshal of some wild old western town.

Sam jumped in his truck and spun his tires furiously in the gravel as he sped out the driveway. I went inside and wrote a check for $1,000 — half what he asked for and five times what he deserved, but a lot cheaper than a stay in the hospital. At least the tile setting was done, I told myself, and we had seen our last of Sam Foster.

Neither turned out to be true, of course. Murphy's law.

36.

Still Looking for Provence

Meanwhile, the search for a perfect local cuisine continued.

Despite our previous experience, the workers on the project insisted that we had not given barbecue a fair chance. We had just gone to the wrong place, on the wrong night, eaten the wrong thing. Maybe we're just the *wrong people,* said I. Maybe our palates aren't sensitive enough. Maybe our sense of gastronomic adventure isn't developed enough. Maybe we don't crave the exotic enough. Maybe we fear arteriosclerosis too much.

Still, at the urging of all those who depended on our continued good health for their livelihoods, we agreed to give barbecue another try.

This time, however, we took a guide.

Anne Cauthra was a native, although hardly your traditional southern belle. A diminutive five foot four in spike heels, with her short dark hair cut at a smart French angle, she could have been an art student in Rome or the clerk in a Left Bank bookstore. The only thing she had in common with Scarlett O'Hara was waist size. We had met her when she responded to an advertisement we placed in the *Standard* for a part-time typist and researcher. She was bright, enthusiastic, and at ease around people, and she had a local library card. We hired her on the spot. Little did we know that she would soon become the Virgil of our culinary tour.

"Just look for the log cabin on the right," she said as we drove along a narrow back road toward North Augusta. "It's called the Fitzgerald Chicken Coop." I could hear only the faintest accent, so faint it could have come from anywhere, Texas to Brooklyn. An actress in high school and college, Anne had struggled for years to purge the geography from her voice. "When I'm somewhere else, it disappears," she lamented. "But after I hang around home for a while, it's impossible."

The "log cabin" that sounded so promising turned out to be a huge hangar with seating for about three thousand. Anne told us that this was actually a replacement building. The first Fitzgerald family Chicken Coop — which really *was* built of logs — had burned down some years ago when one of the big barbecue pits got out of hand. The owner, Larry (whom Anne knew personally), had rebuilt it to the same plans, but using concrete this time. The logs on the outside were fake, Anne assured us.

Inside, the Chicken Coop looked a lot like the other barbecue place, only bigger: the same gingham tablecloths, the same wood paneling (fake, of course), the same picnic-style seating. It did have entertainment, however. In the far corner of the room, a cadaverous old man sat on a bench and hummed off-key as his skeletal fingers coaxed a wheezing, halting version of "She'll Be Comin' Round the Mountain" from the tired lungs of an old electric Wurlitzer.

The food, Anne assured us, was even better. She recommended that we try "either the fried chicken sandwich, bone-*in,* or else the CHOKE — a fried CHicken sandwich, bone-*Out,* served with a coKE."

The only empty seats we could find shared a long table with a family of eight: a father, a mother, and six daughters ranging in age from late teens to just out of diapers. All seven females were dressed in floor-length chiffon gowns with spangled collars and spangled ribbons at the back, and all — even the toddler — topped by coronas of blond hair, teased and sprayed into frothy mounds of majestical proportions.

"Gypsies," Anne whispered behind her hand.

Blond gypsies?

The rest of Anne's explanation had to wait until a place at a nearby table opened up. Once resettled safely out of earshot, she told us the whole strange and mesmerizing story of the Irish Travelers.

Like W.C. and the Winter Colony, this clan of outsiders had moved to the area (in the 1950s, in their case) and built their own community of big houses about fifteen miles from

Aiken. We had passed through it on the way to the Chicken Coop. Every house was built of brick, with bars at the windows and a statue of the Madonna (not the singer) in the front yard. They had to be big because they typically housed two or three generations together. "When the gypsies build a house," Anne explained, "they can't live in it for the first year or two. They cover the windows with aluminum foil to ward off evil spirits and live in a trailer in the driveway."

How did they earn enough money to build those sprawling brick compounds that they couldn't live in?

"They go door-to-door offering to install linoleum floors and carpets," said Anne, "or do minor repairs, roofing, paving driveways, that sort of thing."

How much money could there be in that?

"Plenty," said Anne, "if you collect deposits and never do any work." That was the secret to their success. They'd just keep knocking on doors until they found somebody who needed work done — almost any work, it didn't matter what since they didn't plan to do it anyway — make a low bid, collect a deposit, then disappear. Or they might actually do the work, in a half-assed way with the cheapest materials, then collect their money and skip town before the toilet overflowed, the kitchen floor buckled, or the new driveway melted away. Other times, they didn't bother with any charade and just robbed the house the first time the owners stepped out.

Needless to say, with business practices like those, they had to do a lot of traveling. Hence the name. The search for new suckers, er, customers — the elderly were favorite targets — took them all over the country. Everywhere, in fact, except Aiken, which was considered too close to home and where locals, like Anne, could spot them coming a mile away.

Anne, in fact, was something of an expert on Irish Travelers, especially their murky financial dealings. Before working for us, she had been a teller at the local bank where most of the clan kept their money. "A list of gypsy financial tips would read like this," said Anne: "One, Cash. Two, Cash. Three, Cash. Four, More cash. The men would go off on these long trips all over the country and wire cash back to their wives. Like twenty-five thousand dollars a week. And this was just for their wives to *spend*. It didn't include what they were pocketing."

Where did all that cash go?

Not into the bank, according to Anne. Gypsies didn't like banks — or, more particularly, they didn't like the IRS eavesdropping on their bank business. Occasionally, they would bring cash in to deposit, but always in amounts under the federal limit that could be deposited in one day without reporting to the IRS. Sometimes they brought cash in to be laundered — literally. "The wives would bring in these big wads of bills," Anne told us, "and they would stink like crazy. Naturally, I asked why. They said they put the cash in empty gasoline cans for safekeeping. Right. Safe from what? A fire? Sometimes the cash was so old it was falling apart. You could barely make out the denominations. Counting a wad of it was like peeling a moldy onion."

The Irish Travelers had all kinds of ways of throwing sand into the machinery of tax collection. They all used the same names — everyone was either a Carroll, a Riley, or a Murphy — and always got their mail at post office boxes, sometimes sixty or seventy names to a box. Any tax or bill collector looking for "Pat Murphy" could easily find ten men with that name, all with the same address.

And maybe even the same Social Security number. Anne told us the story of a woman who called the bank to find out if a CD had matured. "I knew this was a scam," she recalled. "They would buy CDs using the Social Security numbers of minor children so they wouldn't have to pay tax on the interest. They bought only in small amounts, of course, so the IRS never heard about it. So this woman is calling to see if one of the CDs she bought in her kid's name has matured. Only, when I punch the Social Security number she gives me into the computer, two names pop up. Well, that's not supposed to happen — it's a federal violation, you know — so the system goes bonkers, blows a fuse, and shuts down. Usually, they were pretty slick about what they did, but we caught them on that one."

Just then, one of the extravagantly maned girls at the next table got up and headed past us to the dessert bar. She was followed quickly by all of her sisters except the toddler. Every one had the identical little shuffling step ("It's the tight skirts," Anne informed us), and every one made the same noise as she passed — the jangling and clunking of armloads and earloads of metal and pasteboard jewelry. Anne ducked and winced as they passed behind her. "I used to hate it when gypsy women came in the bank," she said in an angry whisper after the parade had passed. "The children were always obnoxious and uncouth. One little girl used to come up to the window and pound on the counter, 'I'm waiting. Get me my coin wrappers.' I wanted to slug her."

My eyes were still on the floats. They had gathered around the pie table like lionesses around a watering hole. "How do they get their hair to stand up like that?" I asked Anne.

"Blow drier, teasing, forty-five minutes every day, and hair spray," she said. "*Lots* of hair spray. So much hair spray that it clumps in your hair, and shampoo won't get it out. So much hair spray that you have to use baking soda to get rid of it."

I looked at Anne in amazement. Svelte, stylish, continental Anne. How did she know all that?

"I used to porch my hair."

Porch?

"That's what they call it. 'Porched hair.'" She held her hand up to her forehead, palm out, fingers curved forward. "Get it? Porched. The boys used to joke, 'What do you say to a girl with porched hair? "Hey, hon, got a building permit for that thing?"'"

"And dyed, too. Didn't I tell you? In my high school graduation picture, I was a blonde with hair out to here." She held her hands a foot out from her smart, dark French cut. It was hard to imagine that the intervening space had once been filled with hair.

"And let me tell you, it was a pain in the ass. You had to wash it before you went to bed. And with all that spray, just let some boy try and run his fingers through it. No way. But it was really more a rebellion thing than a boy thing. My mother wouldn't let me wear it as high as I wanted. The gypsy girls always had the biggest hair."

In fact, according to Anne, the gypsy girls were the class leaders in a lot of ways: the first to wear sexy clothes ("They looked like Vegas hookers in seventh grade"), the first to don jewelry ("Ditto"), the first to put on makeup and the first to pierce their ears ("Ditto and ditto"). They were also the first in a more important way. "I remember sitting around with my friends in sixth grade," Anne recalled, "talking about how excited we were to be going to junior high the next year. And a gypsy girl said she didn't have to go to junior high because she was getting *married*."

Gypsy marriages were always arranged, of course, and always to other gypsies. Anything else was scandal. Anne had once heard a story about a local woman who made a fortune selling Mary Kay cosmetics to gypsy women (not hard to imagine after surveying the seven stuccoed faces at the next table) and then *fallen in love with a gypsy man*. The man couldn't divorce his wife — gypsies, being nominally Catholic, don't believe in divorce — so what did he do? He claimed his wife was insane and committed her to an asylum where she was never heard from again. But he still couldn't marry Ms. Mary Kay. Even when his wife died years later, he couldn't marry her, so strong was the ban on outside marriages.

Didn't that cause problems? we wondered. Inbreeding and all?

"Everybody knows that their teenage girls go down to the truck stops to bring fresh blood into the camp," Anne explained. "If you go down to the Smile Station at the Belvedere exit off I-20 some night, you'll probably see one of these girls there." She motioned toward the row of porched heads just as they got up to leave. For a moment, the jangling and clunking almost drowned out the wheezing death throes of the organ.

On their way to the door, two of the older girls — they looked to be about fifteen or sixteen — stopped directly behind Anne. For one awful minute, I thought they had heard our conversation. Then I saw they were looking down at Anne. "Excuse us," one of them said, bringing Anne's head spinning around in panic. "We love your earrings." Anne tried to hide the look of horror that passed reflexively across her face. The earrings were, well, big. And colorful. Anne turned red with embarrassment. "You mean you *r-r-really* like them?" she stammered.

"We *love* them," the girls gushed.

After just a moment of awkward indecision, Anne reached up, fumbled the earrings off, and handed them up to the girls behind her. "If you love them that much," she said, "I want you to have them." The girls squealed and giggled but didn't hesitate a second before grabbing the earrings and heading for the door. Once they disappeared and she had a chance to catch her breath, Anne explained: "If *they* like 'em, I don't want 'em."

And what about the food? Ah, the food! How can I describe it? Or better yet, how would Peter Mayle describe it? The main course was the barbecue itself, a wickedly tangy but enigmatic meat *ragout* — a paradox achieved by carefully shredding the meat to disguise its true origin, and adding an adventurous *frisson* of salt. To accompany this, we chose a quaint local corn dish. The chefs — actually a team of men on loan from the South Carolina Board of Corrections — had procured several magnums of corn from the local market, which they opened with a colorful ceremony involving cigarettes and chewing tobacco. The corn was allowed to simmer languorously in a subtle broth of local water seasoned with another *frisson* of salt and a *brouette* of butter for exactly as long as it took the chefs to conclude their ceremony with the traditional coughing and spitting. Nor could we resist the big, bright-blue bucket full of a glossy-brown bean dish that beckoned us from the far end of the gingham-covered buffet table. How did they achieve that pungent aroma? we wondered. Later, back in the kitchen, we asked the *sous* chef, a huge man with a gallery of tattoos on his upper arm, and eyebrows that met. He seemed complimented by our curiosity. *"Git the hail outta mah kitchin!"* he told us enigmatically. The meal was served with a delightfully light, fluffy bread, baked in loaves of an ingenious rectangular shape, and an effervescent dark-brown beverage bottled regionally.

37.

Real Men Love
Jesus

When we came to Aiken, we found God.

Everywhere.

There were churches, it seemed, on every corner. (Someone told us Aiken had more churches per capita than any community in America, and we could believe it.) In town, of course, were the usual grand old suspects — Catholic, Episcopal, Methodist, Presbyterian, and about a dozen Baptist — with their columns and pediments and classic bell towers, shaded by stately trees and nuzzled by ancient graveyards. Out of town, however, the pitch was more, well, contemporary. Almost every church had its own mar-

quee, like the cineplex at the mall, on which black-plastic letters spelled out the eternal-truth-of-the-month to passing motorists, turning a casual trip to the grocery store, or almost anywhere else, into a gauntlet of inspiration: "Life Is a Lottery, Win with Christ," "Come Share Sunday Supper and Make Friends with the Lord," or simply, "Jesus Lives."

Clearly, we were not in Sodom-and-Gomorrah-on-the-Hudson anymore, Toto.

Even stranger to our jaded eyes was the casual use of religion in the service of commerce — "Taking the Lord's name in gain," we called it. Pest-control trucks emblazoned with "Jesus Loves the World"; business cards with "Jesus Is Lord," in bright-red letters, between the address and the fax number; a sign over the shampoo sink in a barbershop exhorting patrons to "Praise the Lord." Some merchants, it seemed, couldn't sell a pack of cigarettes, rent a video, or launder a shirt without invoking the deity. Jesus was not only their personal savior, he was their financial adviser and marketing consultant. A local jeweler's sign routinely mixed sale announcements with devotional messages.

SPECIAL!
DIAMOND TENNIS BRACELETS
15% OFF
JESUS LOVES YOU

But our favorite was a roadside sign for a beauty shop/massage parlor:

JESUS IS LORD!
YES, WE HAVE THIGH CREAM

Our nurseryman, Ron Gengrich, wore his religion on his sleeve — literally: a small fish patch on the shoulder of his uniform, just above the emblem of his company, a palmetto palm (the state tree), right between the first two words of the company name: "Big G Nursery & Septic Service."

But Ron's devotion didn't stop there. Not at all. In fact, religion was just about all Ron talked about. He could not get through a discussion of boxwoods or camellias or fertilizer mix without letting us know that he went to church every Sunday, real regular. Or that he read the Bible every night — it was his favorite book, couldn't tire of it, no, never could. Or that he never, never, never — I repeat, *never* — cheated on his wife.

Not that he wasn't tempted. Lord, how he was tempted. One day, while planting some cherry bushes to fill in a hedge, Ron filled Steve in on just *how* tempted. It seemed he had once been propositioned by his sister-in-law — "a real looker, with a perky little rear end." He was tempted, yes sir. Sore tempted. But he thought of his wife and his kids and his place with the Lord, he said, and just turned her down flat. Couldn't do it, no, never could.

About a month later, Ron returned to Joye Cottage to re-place some dead boxwoods in the formal garden, and we got Act II of The Temptation of Ron.

"Ah was changin' some shrubs for a motel outside town," he told us, the sour look on his face betraying the moral quandary to come. "Now, it's owned by this Indian couple — you know, like from *India*. And the wife is a real pretty gal, with a lot of skin showin' under that Indian thang she wears all the time." Ron's round, brown eyes began to get narrow and dewy. He was a plain but not unat-tractive man who had obviously been a real looker himself once, probably in high school. As he told us his story, he was sitting on the steps leading from the box garden up to the ballroom porch. I noticed his knee beginning to twitch in a fast, pistonlike motion, faster and faster as his story spilled out in ever more heated spurts.

"Anyway, there Ah am, and she calls me into her bed-room. Ah mean, this is her *bedroom*. And Ah'm thinkin', 'Does she have plants in there or sumpin'?' But when I get in there, there's no plants. It's just her and me, me and her. And she says to me, 'Ah thank you're real good lookin'.' To *me!* And Ah'm standing there and Ah says, 'What about your husband?' 'Oh, my husband,' she says, real disgusted-like. 'He's a worthless son of a gun. He jest sets in his room watchin' dirty Indian movies on his VCR all day long,' she says. 'I need a real man for a change.' That's what she tells me. That's what she tells *me!*"

By this time, Ron was up and pacing the ballroom porch, back and forth in his big, muddy boots. "It was all Ah could do to turn the lady down. Ah thought of mah wife and mah kids and mah place with the Lord, and Ah told her to get herself a new man to put in her shrubs. Ah mean, a man can only take so much temptation, if ya know what Ah mean."

The next time we called Ron to have some planting done, his phone was disconnected. From the nurseryman we found to replace him (who had a "Praise the Lord" bumper sticker on his truck), we heard Act III of Ron's story.

It seemed Ron's wife had caught him in bed with another woman — her sister. Following local custom, she ran to the closet, grabbed a gun, and tried to blow his head off — or, as the nurseryman put it, "tried to shoot him dead." Lucky for Ron, his wife was a bad shot. He ran, and she gave chase, firing five more rounds in his general direction. His last words as he jumped in his truck and headed out of town, never to be seen again:

"A MAN CAN ONLY TAKE SO MUCH TEMPTATION."

38.

On the Post Office Steps

On a bright Sunday afternoon in November, we were walking downtown in shorts and T-shirts enjoying a day off from
work and congratulating ourselves on the wisdom of leaving New York (which was just digging out from its first big
snowstorm of the season) when we saw a crowd gathering
around the old post office at the corner of Laurens Street
and Park Avenue, the main intersection in town. Both
streets had been roped off by police. Was it a demonstra-
tion? For what? Against what? What was there in Aiken to
protest?

Arrayed around the steps of the old post office, a wonderful neo-Jeffersonian redbrick building complete with rotunda, cupola, and grand arched windows, we saw half a dozen knots of people, each knot dressed in a different color robe: deep purple here, magenta by the rail, green and gold next to each other in one of the blocked-off streets. The faces in some knots were all white, in others, all black. Every once in a while, the breeze would catch their robes and billow them into full bloom, so that each little knot of robed figures became a kind of blossom, with pistils of black or white and petals of purple or magenta cast on the dark pond of asphalt before the post office steps.

Several hundred people stood around them, forming a circle of black and white faces that fell loosely over the rectilinear terrain of the intersection. On the broad, grassy medians that ran down the middle of both streets, a few spectators had opened lawn chairs or spread out blankets. At the fringes of the crowd, behind a wall of backs, children played. On the median nearest us, a little white boy and a little black girl, both about five, engaged in an intense game of tag around a pear tree, oblivious to history.

By the time the first blossom, the purple one with white pistils, broke into petals and rearranged itself into rows on the post office steps, we knew what we had stumbled on: Several local church choirs were giving a joint concert. Just then, a multicolored huddle of robes near the rail parted to reveal a stout woman in beehive hair sitting at a dwarfed beechwood upright. She carefully opened her music and began to play. A second later, the piano's tiny, tinny sound, a sound that seemed much farther away than it was, reached our accidental "seats" fifty feet away. When the choir began to sing, in a high, feathery voice, that sound, too, seemed impossibly far away, like the radio of a distant neighbor in an apartment building heard through a heating duct. The song was "Jesus Beneath My Wings," or at least that was the refrain that the sopranos kept repeating, and they were the only voices I could hear. When even they died away, a wave of polite applause drifted over the crowd.

The purple blossom was followed by the magenta blossom, another flower with white pistils. They, too, stood stone-still in their places on the stone steps. They, too, produced a distant, floating sound, like an echo by itself, singing a folksy, contemporary version of "Nearer My God to Thee." They, too, filed off the steps to the rustle of polite applause.

Before the next group could take its place, Steve and I turned to leave.

"Don't leave *now!*" came a voice from behind us.

It was Mordia. I recognized his voice even before we saw him. But when we turned around, the only thing recognizable was the extravagant topiary on his head. The rest of him, from his neck to his toes, was draped in a magnificent robe of opalescent green. Every shade of green, from lime to moss, emerald, jade, forest, hunter, spring, kelly — they were all there, in constantly changing moiré patterns, as the November light played across and Mordia moved inside this shimmering, satiny gown of many colors.

Without another word, he brushed past us and headed across the street toward the post office steps. Suddenly, from everywhere in the audience, men and women in opalescent green robes and dark faces broke through the ring of onlookers and converged on the steps. Before long, they were fifty strong, their gorgeous robes quivering a thousand colors in every passing breeze. A tiny, elderly woman with fingers like twigs commandeered the piano, opened its top, settled onto the bench, rolled up the sleeves of her robe, then turned to her director for the signal to start. At the wave of his arm, her fingers hit the keys.

A second later, the sound rolled over us like thunder.

The choir clapped and swayed and shimmered with delight as the music in those bony hands shook the ground and rattled the grand old Jeffersonian windows.

In another second, the audience was on its feet, clapping and swaying. Old men lifted themselves onto their canes; old women leapt out of their lawn chairs, clapping and swaying. Even the little children, arrested in midflight, silenced in midsqueal, ran to join the clapping and swaying as this little twig of a woman rocked the old post office with the rhythm of the ages.

And then they began to sing. *"His love lifts me up, up, up!"* The sound virtually exploded out of them. Like a mighty wind, it swept across the intersection and spun the audience into a thrill of jubilation. With each *"up!"* their voices only grew stronger, impossibly stronger. The sound wasn't like any choir I had ever heard or sung in before: all careful balance, clear harmonies, and cool sonorities. This was fire to their ice. Singers like to talk about where a voice is produced: in the head, in the throat, or in the chest. These voices came from a different place entirely, a place not on any voice teacher's chart.

Then, suddenly, the music shifted. In a great rumbling transition, an earthquake of harmony and rhythm, the piano lady raised the key and doubled the tempo. The choir shouted and stomped its approval, double-timed its clapping, and tightened its swaying to a fervent shaking. The embankment of electric-green robes quivered in the sunlight like a single, huge banner caught in a rippling wind, and from it arose a single, mighty voice, higher and stronger than ever, *"His love lifts me up!"*

The crowd was transported. "Up!" somebody shouted in response.

"Up!" the choir rejoined.

"Up!" the audience encouraged.

"UP!" the choir roared.

I saw Mordia in the top row, shaking like a power line downed in a storm.

Suddenly, a single voice, a woman's voice, launched over the choir and hung in the sky above it, impossibly high for impossibly long, before exploding in a fireworks of melisma. *"His love . . ."* It was coming from a woman just two rows in front of Mordia, an attractive, middle-aged woman wearing her hair in a bun and her glasses on a chain.

"His love . . . ," the choir exhorted her again.

"His love . . . ," she responded, even more fervently and more elaborately.

"Lifts me up . . . ," the choir sang.

". . . It lifts me . . . ," she agreed, and then, after a great gulp of air, on a note that reached heaven and lasted an eternity, *"up!"*

Underneath her, the choir had time for one last, drawn-out *"lifts me up"* before resolving itself in a jubilant, judgment-day stillness. The soloist, too, spun out her last golden thread, and the piano lady came to rest with a tectonic chord in the left hand and a jazzy flourish in the right, until finally, the sound of the crowd's shouts of delight drowned out the echoing last chords from the post office steps.

With the crowd still whistling and stamping, the singers broke up just as they had gathered, scattering and dissolving into the crowd, and another group began to take their place. Mordia rushed past us, already tugging at his robe, barely pausing as we tried to congratulate him. "Don't you plan to stay and watch the next group?" Steve asked.

Mordia wheeled around and looked at the group of gold robes and white faces taking the steps. We could see him struggling with an answer even as he struggled with his opalescent robe. He managed an uneasy smile but never could bring himself to say what we were all three thinking: Why do white folks bother?

39.

The Right White

And then the rains came.

Not that I'm complaining. In fact, for our first nine months in Aiken, the weather was incomparable: a balmy, sunny fall that reached past Thanksgiving and an equally long, languid spring that arrived around Valentine's Day and never left. Between the two, it snowed only once, in early December, and then only enough to dust the grass and bushes — just enough to get a picture of Joye Cottage in the snow for our Christmas cards — and was gone by noon.

But then the rains came.

The rain in South Carolina may not have a name, but it

deserves one — and not a romantic French one, either; something Anglo-Saxon and unprintable. We thought we had seen rain when hurricane Hugo blew through the area only a month after our arrival. But that was a sprinkle compared to what came in December, just as work on the house reached the penultimate stage: pandemonium. Our picturesque clay street, so soft on horses' hooves, turned into a quagmire that even Maniacal Manny's heavily armed four-by-four couldn't cross. Deliveries had to be hand-carried from the nearest paved road. And we're not talking pizza, either. We're talking thousands of board-feet of lumber and thousands of pounds of plaster, all of it portered by Mordia's crew, board by board, bucket by bucket, in the pouring rain, over soft ground.

And still the rains came. So hard that the basement filled with water over the walk boards; one by one, the steps at the bottom of the black hole disappeared underwater, and the frogs and snakes danced in the darkness. So hard that the pool overflowed and we awoke one morning to an entire courtyard filled with several inches of water. For just a moment, it was quite beautiful — Joye Cottage as some magical maharajah's palace floating among the lily pads of an Indian lake — until we realized that it was undermining our foundations, rotting our porches, and cascading into our basement. So hard that our new roof leaked, our new downspouts backed up, our new gutters overflowed, and I, as the one who had overseen the roofers' work, found myself walking the slick-as-ice shingles in the pouring rain, soaked to the skin, making angry notes while trying not to slip and kill myself.

And still the rains came. Inside the house, work ground

to a soggy standstill. Plaster refused to dry. Lath rusted. The carpenters continued to work, but in the saturated air, boards curled and warped and grew by a quarter of an inch. When the rain ended and the sun returned, almost every piece of wood cut during the deluge had to be refitted or filled in. The slowdown in work did have one benefit, however; it gave us an excuse to fire Sick Nick. But even that did little to lift the pall of glumness that fell over the workers as gray week followed gray week, and the water in the basement rose higher and higher, and the mud sucked harder and harder at their boots. Like squabbling siblings trapped together in the house on a rainy weekend, they communicated increasingly in glowering silences and homicidal glances.

And then, just when we thought things couldn't possibly get any worse, the painters arrived.

The first to appear was Lee Lawrence, a high school dropout from Augusta who came with good references and an even better price. Never having picked a painter before, we didn't know what else to go on. (Steve noticed that when he came from another job for the interview, he didn't have any paint on his overalls. So at least he was neat.) A big commercial painting contractor from Columbia wanted twice as much for the job, and the half-dozen freelancers we interviewed all reminded us of Anne's stories about Irish Travelers. We narrowed the field by eliminating anyone who insisted on being paid in cash, in advance, and anyone with the last name Murphy.

That left Lee.

Lee was a redneck and quick to tell you so — although he looked more like Donny Osmond than Gomer Pyle. On

Friday nights, he went into Augusta to get "tore outta dah frame," which we understood to mean drunk. After lunch, he was always "full as a tick." His reaction to a neighbor with a recent face-lift: "She looks lahk she trahd to eat an apple through a barbed-wahr fence." And our favorite, said in moments of frustration or anger, "Oh, go pee up a wet rope," although we were never sure exactly what it meant.

Curiously, no one enjoyed a good redneck joke more than Lee. "How does a redneck find a date?" he asked at our very first meeting. "He goes to a family reunion!" and then laughed his big, amiable laugh. "How do you know you're a redneck?" he asked. "When your rich uncle buys a house and you have to go help him take the wheels off!" He also showed us his tattoos: one on each forearm, one on each shoulder, one on each pectoral, and one on his back. All were of eagles and snakes and variations on same (winged snakes, fanged eagles, etc.). "They're mah own desahn," he said proudly, and offered to design one specially for me.

It was only after hiring him that we discovered Lee's most endearing habit: He always agreed with you. No matter what the circumstances, no matter how easy the truth might be, or how obvious, he always told you exactly what he thought you wanted to hear. When would he finish painting the salon? "When do you want it done, Mr. Smith?" he would say, bobbing his head up and down. "By the end of the week? End of the week it is, then." Of course, at the end of the week the salon wasn't finished, but Lee was still agreeable. "When do you need it? Middle of next week? Consider it done." It got to the point where he would agree with what we said even before we said it. A typical conversation:

"Should we use . . ."

"Absolutely."

"Latex or . . ."

"Latex."

". . . acrylic?"

"Acrylic."

"Which?"

"Whichever." And his head would bob like one of those figures in the back window of a '72 Pontiac.

Naturally, we trusted Lee with all of our most important decorating decisions. Like what color to paint the walls.

"White?" we asked.

"White," said Lee.

But *which* white? Before we left New York, an article had appeared in the *Times* that asked the same question; a question on the lips of decorators throughout the *House & Garden*-speaking world; a question that haunted the post-modernist, post-Bauhaus era: "Which White Is the Right White?" With the Death of White — also known as white-white or ceiling white, and the color of our New York apartment — we found ourselves adrift on a foamy sea of whites — Lace, Linen, Chalk, Atrium, Chantilly, Eggshell, Ecru, Macaroon Bisque, Silver Lining, SoHo Smoke, Boston Creme, Oriental Silk, and on and on through fifty more. Did we follow the lead of the White House, with Duron Whisper White? Or Carnegie Hall, with Fuller O'Brien Little Deer White?

"Whichever," said Lee.

We explained our dilemma to the manager of a local paint store.

"I'm busy," he said.

Too busy for *this?* We couldn't believe it. Too busy to explore the differences between Lace, Linen, Chalk, Atrium, Chantilly, Eggshell, etc., etc.?

Finally, grudgingly, and only after we told him we had sixty rooms to paint, he agreed to take every shade of white in his store and paint samples of them all on boards. "You guys take the boards back to your house and hold them up to the wall. See which one you like. Who cares what the hell you call it." Fair enough.

For the next week we held up every board, twenty in all, in every possible light — bright and dim, sun and moon, direct and indirect, incandescent and fluorescent — at every time of day and night, in every kind of weather except snow. We squinted at whites with a touch of gray (too dingy), whites with a touch of yellow (too common), and whites with a touch of blue or green or pink or violet (too weird: a Manhattan decorator's career statement, but *sixty rooms* of it?).

Every time we showed Lee a board, his response was the same: "Whichever."

After seven days, we were seeing white. But we still didn't know *which* white. So Steve proposed another solution. Why not pick a room that was painted a shade of white we liked, and then find out what shade it was? Easy enough. And we both knew exactly which room to pick: the scene of our farewell to New York, the living room of Esther Feinberg's fabulous penthouse apartment in the El Dorado, the one with the spectacular Picassos and Matisses on the walls and the spectacular views of Manhattan out the windows. *That* was the right white.

"I don't really know the exact formula," Esther told Steve when he called. "My painter mixes it up himself. It's a custom color."

Oh, great! We finally find the right white and we can't get the formula! Sensing our frustration, Esther offered to ask her painter for the recipe. "But he may consider it a professional secret," she cautioned. Two eternal, agonizing days later, she called back. The painter was willing to share his formula with us — *but* . . . we had to promise on pain of death not to share it with another soul.

It would die with us, we pledged.

"It's one thirty-second of a teaspoon of Raw Sienna," Esther revealed, lowering her voice to a whisper for fear, I suppose, that Benjamin Moore might have tapped the line, "in a gallon of plain white."

At the crack of the next dawn, we raced to the paint store and ordered twenty cans of acrylic white, all mixed to a "special formula," which we passed to the manager on a folded slip of paper and demanded that he return. To our astonishment, he called later the same day to say our order was ready. But when we arrived to pick it up, we found twenty cans of Sherwin Williams Dover White paint clearly labeled, "factory-mixed."

"But we ordered a custom color!" Steve cried in anguish. *"A thirty-second of a teaspoon of Raw Sienna in a gallon of white!"*

"And that's exactly what you got," said the manager, rolling his eyes in exasperation. "A thirty-second of a teaspoon of Raw Sienna in a gallon of white. That's exactly the formula of our most popular color, Dover White. We got a couple hundred more cans in the warehouse if you need 'em."

40.

The Painter's Black Eye

Painters, we soon discovered, travel in packs, and before long, Lee had brought a retinue of retainers to Joye Cottage, all, it seemed, with slight variations on the same name. There was a Lonnie, a Lynne, a Lannell, and a Landon. Coincidence? Hardly. They all had the same last name, too: Lawrence. The Lawrence cousins. They could have been a circus act: The Painting Lawrences.

Once the weather cleared and plaster began to dry again, more and more rooms needed painting. Eager to make up for all the lost time, we, of course, readily agreed to Lee's suggestion that hiring more painters would speed the job along when, in fact, exactly the opposite was true. The more painters we hired, the more radios blasted out country music, the louder and more complex grew the shouted conversations about intrafamilial strife, the less work got done. It seemed Lee's cousin Lonnie was having trouble with his wife, Lauretta, who also happened to be the sister of Lynne, Lonnie's second cousin four times removed (some branches of the family tree appeared to be corkscrew). Lonnie spent his weekends hunting and shrimping with Lynne instead of being home with Lauretta. Lauretta wanted a baby. Lonnie wanted a new boat.

One day, Lonnie Lawrence appeared after the lunch break with a saucer-sized black eye.

"What happened?" I asked, naturally curious. Earlier that morning, he had looked fine.

"Me and my wife, Lauretta, we had an argument," said Lonnie with a big goofy smile, which seemed to be a Lawrence family trait. "So she throwed a chair at me."

As far as I was concerned, this explanation raised more questions than it answered. Like, "When exactly did this incident take place?"

"Last night," said Lonnie.

Like, "Then, why wasn't your eye black *when you came to work this morning?*"

"I dunno," said Lonnie with another big goofy grin.

Like, "*How* did it happen?"

"Well, I told Lauretta I wanted to go huntin' with my cousin Lynne, and she said she was pregnant and she wanted me around the house more, and I said I was goin', and she jest picked up the chair and throwed it at me."

Lonnie apparently found this story more respectable

than the truth, which, we later learned, was that Lynne punched him out for bad-mouthing his sister, Lonnie's wife, Lauretta. Clear?

Wait. There's more. It turned out that Lynne had accused Lannell Lawrence, Lonnie's third cousin five times removed, of dealing drugs (another Lawrence family trait) on the work site and had threatened to bring this to our attention. Lynne was doing this not because he had any particular objection to drugs, which he, like most of the Lawrence clan, happened to enjoy, but because he had an objection to Lannell, who, despite the fact that he followed Lynne in the strict family pecking order, was trying to install himself as the head of the Painting Lawrences as soon as Lee bailed out to take a better-paying job with that big commercial painting outfit in Columbia. That was an additional bone of contention in the fierce fistfight that erupted in the basement during lunch that day when Lynne landed a big right cross in Lonnie's eye socket.

We heard about this title match, naturally, not from one of the Lawrence cousins, who, despite all their feuding, maintained a kind of perverse family loyalty by upholding Lonnie's slanderous account of Lauretta's avant-garde approach to interior decoration, but from Mordia, who referred to this upheaval in the white ranks of the painters as "the thrilla in vanilla."

Meanwhile, of course, the painting fell further and further behind. Lee suggested we hire *more* painters, which we did, including another cousin, Lionel, who, unbeknownst to us, had just been released from prison after serving a multi-year sentence for drug smuggling.

41.

Three Horsewomen
of the Apocalypse

Then one day, in this chaos of country music and criminal longings, three women appeared on horseback. Steve and I had just escaped onto the porch for a breath of nonacrylic air when we saw them riding toward us, out of the cloud of red-clay dust that hung over our street during dry spells. At the end of the driveway, they reined their horses to a stop and dismounted as quickly and nimbly as cats. As the dust settled and I saw more clearly their impossibly trim figures and crisp, eighteenth-century clothing, something about them struck me as vaguely familiar. Then I recognized it: They looked like the painted cast-iron jockeys that stood

262 • ON A STREET CALLED EASY

with outstretched arms beside front doors all over Aiken, including our own.

The rider in the middle strode forward. It was Margo Ullman Stanford, she who had tried to warn us away from Mrs. Johnson, the Anti-Dust, with the blunt assessment, "Take her if you want her, but she makes my skin crawl!" She and her two statuesque companions had just returned from a hunt (foxes, that is), and they wanted to talk to us.

What do you say to a woman with a hunting whip?

"No, no, no!" she corrected. "It's a hound crop."

She approached, striding like Lord Mountbatten in her laceless black calfskin boots. How did she get them to glow like that? I wondered. Not like patent leather, but like an old library book caressed by a thousand hands. Polish?

"No, no, no," she corrected. "You don't polish waxed calf, you *bone* it. With the shinbone of a deer." She slapped the plaited thong of her hound crop against her canary-yellow pants.

"No, no, no, not pants, *britches*." And not just plain old britches, either, but melton-cloth britches with suede knee patches, tight at the calf and flared at the thigh. "Some people wear them tight in the thigh," she sniffed, "but I like the traditional hourglass shape." A white stock (tie) was pinned to the standing collar of her hunting shirt under a canary-yellow waistcoat — "pronounced WESScut," she warned — with a melton front and a tattersall silk back.

I asked if I could see the back.

Her mouth dropped open in astonishment. "Hah!" she yelped. "You mean take off my coat?"

"Don't you take off your coat when you get hot?" I ventured. "It must get hot sometimes when you ride in the woods."

"Take off my coat? *Take off my coat?*" The indignation ricocheted around her face before finally escaping in another high-pitched *"Hah!"*

The coat was indeed beautiful, if hot; a rich forest green ("no, no, no, *harrier* green") with chamois collar and brass buttons on front, back, and sleeves. Over the gathered blond hair at the nape of her neck, two little black ribbons hung down from her velvet-covered riding hat, and the staghorn handle of her hunting whip — excuse me, hound crop — slipped menacingly back and forth between the crocheted gloves on either hand.

She saw me looking at her gloves. "String gloves don't slip in the rain," she said, arresting the crop handle with a grip that could brake an eight-hundred-pound horse.

She motioned her friends forward until eight of us were standing in a circle: Steve and me, the three women, and the three horses. The latter six were all members of the Aiken Hunt, the oldest and most prestigious social club in town and the second-oldest hunt club in America. The Aiken Hunt had been watching the course of our renovations with keen interest, said Margo, and wondered how far from completion we were.

"It's hard to say," we hedged. (Truth be told, we didn't want to think about it.)

Undeterred, the three horsewomen made the proposal they had come to make. The Aiken Hunt, the oldest and most prestigious social club in town and the second-oldest hunt club in America, would celebrate its seventy-fifth anniversary in January 1990. To mark this historic occasion, the Hunt was planning to give a ball. Not just any ball, of course, but a white-tie extravaganza; the kind of ball that *Town & Country* would send a reporter to cover and a photographer to immortalize, the kind of ball that had not been seen in Aiken since the days of W. C. Whitney. "A ball like they had a hundred years ago!" Margo exclaimed, starting with an elegant sit-down dinner for 250 of the best people-we-know in tailcoats and sequined gowns, followed by an evening of glorious, glittering dancing and revelry accompanied by a New York orchestra and a river of champagne. It would be the social event of the season, of the year, of the decade, of the century!

And they wanted to hold it at Joye Cottage.

In a month.

"Can you do it?" Margo pressed, slapping her crop against her boot for encouragement. "Can you have the house ready?"

It was a flattering request. Especially for newcomers. And, of course, we wanted to be good neighbors.

Steve and I looked around at the loose boards that needed nailing and the acres of alligatored pine that needed scraping; at the piles of ducting still to be snaked through the bowels of the house; at the crates stacked by the kitchen door, crates filled with furnaces and air conditioners, kitchen appliances and bathroom fixtures, electrical panels and plaster moldings; at the leagues and leagues of wire — electrical, security, telephone, cable, stereo, computer — still to be laid in the watery deep we called a basement; at the forest of lumber still to be sawed and shaped and fitted and nailed and sanded and primed and caulked and painted. For

God's sake, *we hadn't even moved the safe yet!* And then we thought about our workers: Eugene, the Ahab of plasterers; Manny, the homicidal carpenter; Dave, the rock-star electrician; whoever replaced Glenn and Mike and Randy as the next security man *du jour;* Darla (Darth) Vader, the telephone lady; Andy, the orchid-growing roofer of Aspen and Chicken-itza; and, of course, the brawling Lawrence cousins.

And then we looked at each other. *In a month?*

"Of course," we said in unison. "It'll be ready."

Part Four All Balled Up

42.

What Is a Ball,
Anyway?

"A ball like they had a hundred years ago!" That's what Margo had said. But what exactly did that mean? What exactly had we gotten ourselves into? The only ball we knew about a hundred years ago (actually, only ninety-two) was the one W. C. Whitney threw for his new bride, Edith, to celebrate her first and only visit to Joye Cottage. It was Christmas 1897. But who would remember that?

"It were snowin'," said Meta as she backed away, in quick, tiny steps, to escape the blast of cold air from the door as we entered. "I 'member 'cause my feets was cold and wet."

Of course, we couldn't be absolutely sure that the party she remembered was the famous Christmas Ball of 1897, but who would argue with Meta? She remembered only that it was December, that there was "a new Miz Whitney in town," and that she was "real little."

In 1897, Meta was six.

"Me and my brothers watched the coaches pull up from

across the street where we's lived," she told us, settling back into a chair beside a space heater in her bedroom at the far end of a hallway filled with old photographs of black men and horses. "We's always watchin' the high life at night. When Mistuh Whitney throws a party, I could hears the music from my room." Ninety-two years later, her room smelled of paper, stacks of old, yellowed paper piled on crippled shelves all around her bed. It smelled of the past.

"We waits till all them folks is inside and then we sneaks up to the windows to see what we could see," she continued. "We was trampin' in the snow in our bare feets and it was the first time I 'member seein' snow. Weren't deep, but sure were cold." Chilled by the memory, she rubbed her warped, mahogany hands together in front of the heater. "So we goes up to the windows where the party was, and they was ice on the glass, I remember. When we pressed our noses 'gainst it, the ice melted, which I thought was a wondrous thing. Then we could watch all them folks dancin'."

And that's where Meta's story ended. All she knew of that famous ball was what she could see from the window through her frosty portal, with the muffled sound of an orchestra floating in the night air around her and the strange, new sensation of snow between her toes.

To find out more about what might have gone on *inside* Joye Cottage that night more than ninety years ago, we trawled the shallow, colorful coral reefs of history: the journals, diaries, and letters of the socialites who attended W.C.'s parties and every florid society-page account we could find of similar soirées. We discovered that guests were always greeted as they alighted from their carriages by liveried footmen and sheltered as they entered by wide awnings lined with the new marvel of the age, electric lights. Whitney greeted every guest personally, always positioning himself at the most strategic and visible spot in any room — although as tall and distinguished as he was, being noticed was never a problem.

The women were dressed in the imperial fashion of the day: gowns of mirror velvet and brocade embroidered with tiny roses in every shade of pink, for example, or white mousseline de soie covered with gold embroidery and set off by silk flowers, petticoats of silver cloth, and trains of scarlet velvet. And, of course, jewelry: strand after strand of it; too much was never enough; pearls and diamonds at the wrist, at the neck, and garlanded in the hair.

The ballroom was filled with the soft glow of a thousand small lights, gathered into bundles like bunches of brilliant white grapes, swathed in taffeta and entwined in swirls of asparagus vine and camellias of pink and white. At each window hung huge baskets of pink begonias weeping long, glossy-green garlands of smilax vines. (W.C. shipped smilax vines from Aiken to all his homes for parties.)

While the guests gathered in the ballroom, armies of servants padded silently through the house bringing dozens of dinner tables, preset with solid-gold service and crystal bowls overflowing with more pink and white camellias, out from their hiding places and arranging them in the salon, the billiard room, the library, the drawing room. At twelve-thirty sharp (that's half-past midnight!), the maître d'hôtel announced, "Supper is served," and the guests glided across the hand-polished floors in search of their assigned places.

As soon as the last diner was seated, a legion of waiters, as many as a hundred — all of them trained at Sherry's in

New York and imported specially for the occasion —
brought on meals fit for royalty: repasts exquisite, sumptuous, incomparable, and interminable. To the shimmering accompaniment of a Hungarian orchestra caparisoned in
brilliant scarlet-and-gold jackets, the courses came. And
came and came. A piquant *Bouillon en Tasse* followed by a
tawny *Terrapin*. Next, a rich, dark, aromatic Canvasback
Duck, followed by subtle, nutty *Poussins Grillés à la Diable*.
The meal finally began to wind down with *Pâté en Croute* and
Salade. For dessert, an embarrassment of riches: *Gâteaux*,
Glace, or *Bonbons*, or all of the above. Seven courses, at least,
and each one accompanied by another brilliant, surprising
wine or champagne chosen personally by Whitney from
wine cellars nearly as endless as his stables.

The final and most fabulous treats, however, came after
the *Café* and *Appolinaris*. It was then that W.C. dispensed his
legendary party favors. For the ladies, fine jewelry was the
rule, or sometimes jeweled satin scarves. For the men, gold
cigarette cases (everybody smoked) or perhaps fine riding
crops decorated with the insignia of the Whitney stables.
But for W.C., gifts were only half the treat. As famous as he
was for the lavishness of his favors, he was even more famous for the cleverness he displayed in giving them. At one
party, guests were startled by the blare of hunting horns as
three full-size papier-mâché horses (named after three of
W.C.'s most celebrated racehorses, Ballyhoo Bey, Prince
Charles, and Kilmarnock) were "ridden" into the ballroom
by jockeys satined in the Whitney colors (pale blue and
chocolate brown) and laden with sacks of gold and jeweled
favors that they distributed to the gaping crowd.

But, of course, the main event of the night was dancing.

Dancing, dancing, and more dancing. Dancing until five-thirty in the morning. Dancing by a small, select group of young revelers (chosen weeks before for their beauty and grace); dancing by the older, richer, statelier guests; dancing the cotillion; choosing partners for dancing — hiding the men in giant paper balloons or the women behind huge fans — all to heighten and extend the sheer, whirligig thrill of dancing. Dancing as a spectacle of pink satin and diamonds and black wool and blue chiffon and pearls and jade velvet and white piqué and gold, all swirling and swirling across the ballroom floor in a hundred blurs of color and laughter.

Just how spectacular were these affairs — these "balls like they had a hundred years ago," as Margo said? After one Whitney bash, a newspaper reporter rhapsodized: "Nothing that money could buy or taste suggest was spared to make a perfect entertainment." Another party made front-page news: "UNPARALLELED IN SPLENDOR," the headline hyperventilated, "The Finest Private Function *Ever!*"

Oh. *That* kind of ball.

In a *month?*

43.
Help!?

Of course, we did have Desmond.

W. C. Whitney may have had a hundred waiters and a legion of liveried footmen and a cohort of cooks, to say nothing of the vast assortment of pot stirrers and dishwashers who attended every great kitchen of the era. But we had Desmond Harris. He came to us, in the wake of the great bakery debacle with Mrs. Johnson, on the recommendation of a neighbor who had heard that we needed "some help" and didn't realize that the kind of help we needed was more on the order of a Marshall Plan.

Desmond wasn't much of a housekeeper. A short man

with a round face, he never just walked anywhere, he sashayed, swinging his hips from side to side, with one hand hooked rakishly over the belt of his apron and the other holding aloft a feather duster with which he beat the air in time to some unseen band. Thus he Carol-Channinged his way around Joye Cottage. If he ever did anything else with that feather duster (left over from Mrs. Johnson's Anti-Dust crusades), I didn't see it. With the rising chaos of construction all around, I rarely had time to think about cleaning. The one time I stopped him in midsashay and asked him to clean some recently painted windows, he informed me that he didn't do windows.

Actually, Desmond turned out to have an extraordinary knack for entertaining. Call him Aiken's answer to Martha Stewart. He could set a table to make the White House proud, arrange flowers like a Japanese master, and serve a dinner as well as any of W.C.'s hundred Sherry's-trained waiters.

And he loved to cook. His very first day on the job, he brought with him an antique wood box, polished by decades of use and filled with dog-eared file cards on which, I assumed, were recorded generations of great old southern recipes. Very promising. So promising that we set up a temporary kitchen, complete with hot plate and countertop oven, so Desmond could work his down-home culinary magic. In fact, I discovered later, the wooden box contained generations of great old southern *cooks* — the names, addresses, phone numbers, and birthdays of every elderly black lady between Aiken and Charleston, all of whom Desmond considered family. If he wanted to make fried chicken, which he did at least three days a week, he went to his box not for a recipe but for a phone number. Every meal required at least an hour and ten minutes of phone conversation: ten minutes to get the recipe and an hour to discuss who in his Rolodex had died since his last call.

This cooking method resulted in two problems, one foreseeable, one not. The first was that Desmond cooked everything in the old southern style — that is, before the invention of health. His fried chicken was indeed delicious, but it left the walls around the hot plate coated in grease, and our stomachs, undoubtedly, in the same condition. If we had any doubts, all we had to do was watch the rate at which the Crisco disappeared. Cooking for only two people, Desmond used up an entire can of Crisco *every week*. Nor did he have any respect for steaming as a form of food preparation. Steaming vegetables wasn't really cooking them, he insisted, more like sending them to the low country for the summer. Vegetables, he believed, deserved to be boiled down to a vitamin-free, sludgelike puree.

The other, less foreseeable consequence of Desmond's *gastronomie geriatrique* was the alarming death rate in his family. We should have known something was wrong when he came to us on his third day at work and asked for a day off and a fifty-dollar advance on his pay to go to the funeral of an "aunt" in Camden, South Carolina. How could we say no? A death in the family was, after all, a death in the family.

But that was just the beginning. The next week, it was another aunt in another small South Carolina town, another day off, and another fifty dollars (always fifty dollars). The next week, for a change, it was an uncle, but everything else was the same. Then a cousin, then another aunt, then a grandfather, then a niece. Sometimes not even a week separated the funerals. By the end of Desmond's first month with us, seven "close relatives" had died. At that rate, his family would be decimated before the year was out.

But somehow the deaths kept coming — always "close relatives" in faraway towns whose funerals he *had* to attend. Soon he had taken off so many days and taken so many advances that he owed us weeks of salary. He would work for a few days, and then, just as he was beginning to catch up, another aunt would sit down to tea with the Grim Reaper. We tried not to show our growing skepticism — a death in the family is, after all, well, a death in the family — but how many more relatives could he have at death's door? With the Hunt Ball looming closer and closer, the needs of the departed were outweighed by the needs of the desperate.

Finally, after the sudden demise of yet another aunt (in

Florence, from asphyxiation; don't ask), we felt compelled to take action. I instructed Desmond to write down on a piece of paper the names of *all* his relatives, no matter how distant or healthy, whose funerals he would feel obliged to attend. Then, as each one checked out — as they inevitably would; and soon, too, probably — we could check them off the list. Sooner or later, we would emerge on the other side of this plague and get a full week's work for a full week's pay.

Even as he was complying with my request, however, Desmond realized that it was already too late for one name on his list. "I forgot Marvin Lee died yesterday," he informed us. "There's gonna be a funeral tomorrow in Batesberg, and I need fifty dollars."

44.

The Last Laugh

Help wasn't the only advantage W.C. had in giving a ball.
Unlike us, he had a house!

And not just any house, either. The French château at the
corner of Fifth Avenue and 68th Street in New York, where
he gave his most lavish parties, would have made Louis
XIV feel right at home. Some of it, in fact, *was* home. Whitney and his personal architect, Stanford White, had plundered palaces and castles all over Europe, including France,
in search of just the right props for New York's premier
party venue: massive bronze and wrought-iron gates from

the Doria palace in Rome; entire ceilings of painted wood from palaces in Florence and Genoa; stained-glass windows from a German cathedral; a huge stone fireplace pried out of a château in Louis XIV's backyard; carved cupids from a palace in Greece; and a banquet table seating a hundred from a monastery in Italy.

And as for the ballroom itself, Whitney couldn't be bothered with anything as messy and unpredictable as a renovation like ours. He just found a room he liked — in a castle in Bordeaux built by one of Louis's marshals, in fact — and *bought* it, lock, stock, and chandelier.

Even when he entertained at Joye Cottage — a *real* cottage, by comparison — W.C. at least had grand reception areas, numerous dining rooms, and a kitchen equipped with the latest in gas cooking and refrigeration, all of it fully furnished and amply heated by a brand-new five-ton boiler and a basement full of coal.

What did we have? A grand reception room filled with stacks of lumber, piles of sawdust, a lathe, and a table saw; a recently replastered dining room that smelled like a hayloft after a heavy rain; a kitchen equipped with the latest in power tools and coffee thermoses — all without a stick of furniture, and stone-cold even on a sunny day because of the greasy spot on the floor where the boiler used to be; and a basement full of black, wiggly water.

Where Whitney had huge bronze chandeliers and hanging silver lamps, we had bare bulbs hung from wires strung like pathetic Christmas lights from the electrical panels in the basement — the only place we could get power. None of the old fixtures worked — or the switches or the plugs. Where Whitney had hand-painted and gilded ceilings, we had a few ceilings of pristine white plaster, and others, like the Weeping Room, still abstract works of art. In some rooms, rubble still fell from above without warning.

Where Whitney had marble floors and mosaic floors and inlaid oak floors, all covered by fabulous Aubusson carpets and sumptuous Persian rugs, we had a wasteland of dust: wooden floors so embedded with the dross of months of sawing and plastering that sweeping and vacuuming were futile. We had to cover them with cardboard just to keep the clouds down. Where Whitney had walls of green onyx and white marble covered with rich, gold-threaded tapestries by Gobelin, Boucher, and Boekel, tapestries once owned by the British and French royal families, we had rooms with stud walls, lathed walls, and half-lathed walls, wet plastered and half-plastered walls, and even some rooms *without* walls — looking like Dresden after the bombing. In one room, which we planned to panel someday, the walls were still just plain plywood — like the inside of the clubhouse my father built for me in the backyard.

Where Whitney had masterpieces of European art everywhere — Tintoretto, Raphael, Fra Filippo Lippi, Lucas Cranach the Elder, Van Dyck, Millet, and a host of English eighteenth-century portraits (no robber baron household was complete without them) — we had only one thing tacked to the walls: sun-faded blueprints. If you squinted hard, you might be able to see what it would all look like, someday.

In fact, our Joye Cottage had one and only one advantage over Mr. Whitney's New York party palace. Despite admirers' predictions that it would remain a Manhattan landmark for centuries, that house, like almost all the other grand mansions along the golden mile of Fifth Avenue, was gone — demolished less than fifty years after it was built.

Joye Cottage, at least, was still standing.

Sort of.

45.

A Night at
the Opera

Three weeks before the Hunt Ball, the project went to red
alert. Whole seasons of *This Old House* were condensed into
every day of breakneck renovation. Carpenters, plasterers,
plumbers, electricians, gardeners, cabinetmakers, appliance
installers, floor refinishers, carpet layers, furniture movers,
heating contractors, and Mordia's merry band of
laborers — sometimes as many as thirty workers at a
time — ricocheted from room to room, often lost or looking
for something. We issued maps to new hires and visiting
workers, but they would lose the maps, then spend hours
retracing their steps looking for them, stumbling over each

other in the halls, piling up in cul de sacs. Our orderly, if desperate, renovation had degenerated into the stateroom scene from *A Night at the Opera*, played out a hundred times a day in sixty rooms.

Plaster was the key. No matter how quickly the carpenters and electricians prepared a room, or how furiously the painters finished it, everything depended on what happened in between. If two Lamborghinis are caught on a narrow street behind a horse-drawn carriage, the horse sets the pace.

And ours was an ornery horse. At first, we tried to encourage Eugene to work faster by casually asking him how long it would take to finish this room or that wing. When that didn't work — his estimates were always wildly optimistic — we tried some less subtle encouragement: "Come to think of it, Eugene, didn't you say this room would be finished a month ago?"

Eugene was not amused. He would scowl down at us from his scaffolding as if to say, "I'm an *artiste*. I can't be bothered with anything so bourgeois as a schedule." In response, Steve noted pointedly that even Michelangelo had Pope Julius II breathing down his neck (or, actually, up his neck).

Finally, with only a few weeks left before the first ball guest rang our doorbell (assuming we could fix the doorbell), we went to Eugene and suggested the unthinkable. "You know, this is such a *huge* job, Eugene, maybe you ought to hire an assistant."

From his reaction, you would think we had suggested he get a sex-change operation. "Impossible. *Impossible!*" he shouted, stamping his big foot so hard on the scaffolding above our heads that the ballroom shook and plaster dust billowed.

"Just for the brown coat?" we ventured.

"The brown coat? *The brown coat!* If the brown coat ain't smooth, do ya know how long it will take me to correct it on the final coat? Do ya know?"

We didn't know, but we could guess.

"And that'll end up costing ya *more* money!"

So we retreated for a few days while the plastering fell further and further behind and the ball loomed closer and closer.

If we couldn't move Eugene, perhaps we could move the safe. Ever since our initial failure to budge it with brute force, we had managed to work around it, bringing supplies in through windows or maneuvering them around it. After a while, we stopped seeing it altogether — a considerable triumph of mind over matter. But now the hall around it needed plastering and painting, and the floor under it, refinishing. Like the proverbial elephant under the carpet, it could be ignored no longer. The safe had to go.

A locksmith quoted us a price of three hundred dollars to do the job, which seemed fair to us. But no sooner had he made the offer than Lucky Dale, the chimney sweep, who had been standing nearby, motioned me aside. "Listen," he said, "I'll give you five hundred for it." Apparently, he thought the locksmith was going to *pay* us, not *charge* us.

After some consideration, I determined Lucky's was the better offer. "Congratulations, Lucky," I said. "The safe is yours. Now, how are you going to get it out of here?"

Lucky stroked his beard as he sized up the monolith. "I'll have to think about that," he said.

We were halfway there, at least.

But for every step forward, it seemed, we took two steps back. Just when we thought the question of "help" was resolved — at least until after the ball — Desmond Harris turned into Tina Turner. Literally. We had heard that Desmond liked to cross-dress, and we had no problem with that, as long as he didn't come to serve at the ball in a short black dress, white apron, and stiletto heels. As far as we were concerned, what he did on his own time was his own business. When he showed us the pictures of himself dressed up as Tina Turner at the local Halloween bash (where he won first prize), we oohed and aahed appreciatively ("Where'd you get that great leather miniskirt?").

But our Tina Turner also had an addiction problem.

We didn't discover it until our phone bills began to top five hundred dollars a month. When we looked, we saw that someone was placing dozens of "900" toll calls. Not to sex lines, either. That, too, we could have understood (although not at eight-thirty in the morning, when most of the calls were placed and precisely the time Desmond arrived for work). No, these calls were to money lines — lotteries for trips to the Caribbean; thirteen tips on how to get rich; how to secure a credit card with no credit record (Secret: Go to the bank and fill out an application). All this sophisticated financial advice, of course, did not come cheap. The credit card wisdom, for example, cost $25 plus $3 a minute. Before long, these get-rich-quick calls added up to real money — more than Desmond's monthly salary. When we showed him the bills, he burst into tears.

Tears or no, we had to let Desmond go. Now, with the

Hunt Ball only two weeks away, we were once again in need of "help."

Desmond's replacement, Marge, wasn't exactly what we had in mind. A huge, ferocious-looking woman whose previous job had been as a warden in a women's prison, Marge had an appetite that was, well, ferocious. No matter how many portions we asked her to make for lunch, we never found a single leftover in the refrigerator. And she never did anything — cooking, cleaning, *anything* — without a sweet potato in her mouth. "These sure are good!" she would mumble enthusiastically as she chawed down on the end of a big orange yam. One night, we placed three-quarters of a birthday cake — a vast chocolate extravaganza with cream-cheese icing — in the refrigerator. The next day at lunch, after a long morning of anticipation, we went to cut ourselves pieces of leftover cake but found the refrigerator empty. We turned to Marge.

"Ain't no cake left," she said authoritatively. "You wanna sweet potato?"

Meanwhile, back at the renovation, the work continued, oblivious to the domestic drama unfolding under the same roof. And sometimes, just plain oblivious. We had been so busy refereeing the painters and cajoling the plasterer that we barely noticed the comings and goings of Darla, the telephone lady. She seemed the picture of competence and confidence in her festooned belt, hard hat, and Carrhart jacket with the corduroy collar turned up. Since giving her the job of wiring the sound system that ran through all the major rooms of the house, we had heard her say exactly two words — "Hey, guys" — in that gum-smacking baritone. Now she was finished and she wanted to get paid.

There was just one problem. We weren't getting stereo sound — not in a single one of the ten rooms Darla had wired. When Steve and I cleared away the rubble and hooked up some equipment to double-check the wiring, we got the same signals out of both speakers. Steve suggested maybe the problem was our hearing; maybe we were just getting older. But a little playing with the balance knob confirmed the worst. We asked Darla for an explanation.

"What's the problem?" she said, smacking her gum hard.

"The problem is we're getting the same signal out of both channels."

Darla looked baffled, and not happy about it. "Hey," she challenged, "it's comin' out of both speakers, ain't it?"

"*That's* not stereo sound!" Steve flared.

Darla, truly uncomfortable and unhappy by now: "It's not?"

Then the realization dawned. Darla, the person we had paid to put in our stereo system, *didn't know what stereo was!*

Which meant the whole house would have to be rewired.

In two weeks.

Which was more time than we had to finish plastering. New-laid plaster, unlike new-laid wires, needs time to dry. And besides, the music for the ball would be live. We could live without stereo sound — but not without walls.

So we screwed our courage to the sticking place and *told* Eugene: Find an assistant. Pronto.

"It's your house," he said, as if he didn't really believe it. "I guess ah can fin' someone," then muttered epithets under his breath for the rest of the day.

The someone he found, Carl, was the son of a husband-and-wife plastering team Eugene had worked with "in the old days" in Florida, and he came with a singular recommendation: "I fahred him from a prev'ous job," said Eugene. Why? "'Cause he back-talked me." Did that cause a problem with Carl's parents? "When his mother heard about it, she picked up a metal pahpe and beat him over the head with it. Follered him all the way home beatin' him with this metal pahpe."

Apparently, the beating didn't do Carl any permanent good. He worked exactly two days and then disappeared. "I don't know what's wrong with him," Eugene lamented. "He's a smart kid."

Carl's replacement was a "walk-on" — literally — from across the street. One day we saw him mowing the grass at a neighbor's house and the next day he knocked on our door looking for work. We asked what he could do. "A little bit of everything," he said, "carpentry, electrical, plumbing, plaster . . ."

The next day he was up on the scaffold with Eugene.

The next afternoon Eugene was stomping up and down the walk boards again, all 225 pounds of him, kicking up clouds of angry dust, testing the envelope of profanity as well as the tensile strength of plywood. "Ya see *that?*" he yelled from high in the air as soon as he saw us in the doorway. "Ya call that a fucking brown coat! Shit! It's wavier than my mother-in-law's thighs! It'll take me a fucking day to even that out!"

The search for an assistant plasterer continued.

Ten days and counting till the Hunt Ball.

And then, on the ninth day, we were sued.

When the summons arrived, I blinked in disbelief. Sam Foster, the tile setter, was suing us for $1,000 — the money we hadn't paid him for the work he didn't do! *Sam Foster!* The depressed divorcé with a taste for sports talk and Little Debbie snack cakes. *Sam Foster!* The school-yard bully against whom I had scored a TKO in the driveway months ago. We hadn't heard from him since then, and I assumed we'd seen the last of him. Now, with less than two weeks left before B-Day, he was taking us to court.

The facts, of course, were clearly on our side. But Steve and I, having graduated from law school, knew that the facts have only a flirting relationship with the law. And we had lived in Aiken long enough to know that in a small town, north or south, neither the facts nor the law are as important as who you know. Or even better, who you're related to. Unfortunately, on that score, our Harvard Law degrees were no match for Sam Foster. The Fosters had been in Aiken so long that the family tree shaded most of the county. There was even a Foster Street. In short, legally speaking, we were screwed.

Obviously, the only thing to do was fight bloodline with bloodline, and since it was too late to marry one of the judge's relatives, we did the next best thing: We hired one. His name was Al Pritchett, and he was related not only to the judge but, inevitably, to Sam Foster as well. When we asked him if this presented a conflict of interest, he just laughed. "If I couldn't take cases against my kin, I couldn't get any work in this town."

With precious hours ticking away, we left the work site to appear in the city courthouse — actually, a converted storefront in an old shopping center — accompanied by Al Pritchett, our "local muscle" (Mordia's phrase). Sam Foster entered after us, his big fists clenched white and that lightning-bolt vein popping up on his forehead again. He came without a lawyer, a real display of home-court arrogance. As soon as we were all seated, but before the judge appeared, Al excused himself. "I'll just be a few minutes," he said as he headed off, we assumed to the men's room.

Five minutes later, he returned. "We can go home now," he said. "It's all worked out." He hadn't been to the men's room, it turned out; he had been *to the judge's chambers!* Deal done. Case closed. And the only money we owed was to him (of course).

The Great Tile Trial was over before it began.

But even in the short time we were gone, chaos had descended. While running a gas line to a furnace in the attic, J.T., the plumber, had accidentally cut a hole in the roof. While trying to run a wire from another attic down to the basement, Dave, the electrician, had accidentally cut a hole in the ceiling of a porch. Manny, the carpenter, had stepped on a big slab of old marble that we had just repaired and broken it in two. Again. Mordia, carrying two fifty-pound bags of plaster, had stepped on a patch of rotten floor in the Weeping Room and fallen through up to his armpits. The paint on the walls in the very first room we painted, the salon, had begun to peel. We hadn't let the plaster dry long enough. "I told you so," said Eugene helpfully. And finally, the first time I visited a bathroom after returning from the courthouse, a piece of Sam Foster's tile fell from the wall and broke — the first of many.

Then, with only five days to go, Eugene brought in Ethan, a fifty-five-year-old plasterer and another of his buddies from "the old country," as Mordia called Florida. Maybe it was the white uniform, like Eugene's, or the mane of white hair, like Eugene's: whatever it was, Ethan seemed like the answer to our prayers. He worked smoothly and efficiently, like Eugene, and quietly, unlike Eugene, and the results, as far as we could tell, were every bit as good as Eugene's. If anything, Ethan was too good. It soon became apparent that he was doing the work faster and better than Eugene himself.

We had thought that a little healthy competition might light a fire under Eugene's flagging work pace. It lit a fire, all right, *in Eugene's eyes.* Ethan worked too quickly, he complained, not giving each coat a chance to dry. Ethan's surfaces were uneven. Ethan's cornices would never stay put. Ethan didn't know how to miter a corner.

The next morning, when we came to work, it was Ethan's turn to pitch a fit. He had found out that we were paying Eugene more than we were paying him. (Eugene had told him, of course.) And he felt cheated. Especially since Eugene worked too slowly, his surfaces were uneven, his cornices would never stay put, and he didn't know how to miter a corner.

With four days left, what else could we do? We gave Ethan a raise.

Eugene went through the roof. The rafters shook and the walk boards bent almost to the floor as he stormed across the scaffolding, shouting how he "wouldn't take this shit anymore, not for one goddamn, motherfucking minute." With that, he clambered down from his aerie and started to pack up his tools (i.e., throw them all into a big plastic bucket) and dismantle his scaffold.

With three days left!

I should have fallen on my knees and begged him to stay.

Promised him anything. If he walked out, all hope of being ready for the ball went with him. Begging was the rational thing to do. But would a rational man have bought Joye Cottage? Would a rational man have agreed to host the Hunt Ball? Would a rational man find himself in this fix? Which meant one thing.

"How dare you walk off this property!" I screamed back. "After all the shit we've taken from you. After all your whining and wailing and bellyaching! After all your promises that it will only take this long and only cost this much, and it always took twice as long and cost twice as much, and *we didn't complain once!* And now *you* want to walk out on *us?* You've got some gall!"

Eugene looked thunderstruck and hurt at the same time, like he couldn't decide whether to hit me or burst into tears. He finally chose the latter. "Ah'm so sorry," he wailed. "You boys have been like sons to me." With that, he threw his arms around me and broke into sobs.

And all I could think about was the minutes ticking by. *Two days*, and we *still hadn't moved the safe!*

I called Lucky in a panic.

The next morning, he assembled his crew in the basement passage. To our surprise, it was just the usual gang: no big laborers hired specially for the task. Our own laborers, who had lost furious wrestling matches with the big safe more than once, laughed when they saw Lucky's beanpole family gathered beside their old nemesis. Mordia referred to them, as he did to any small group of white people, mordantly as the Brady Bunch. I added up their collective weight and realized it was about one fifth of the safe's. If they dropped it, June Bug or Caterpillar or another of Lucky's sons was going to get squashed.

Still, Lucky went about the task with solemn self-assurance. "Let's get this thing on its side," he announced to his sons, all of whom appeared dazed by lifetimes of requests like this one from their father. Using a long crowbar, they wedged a car jack behind the safe and began ratcheting it away from the wall and onto a plywood skid with rollers of plastic pipe underneath. As it descended, they piled timbers on one side to keep it from falling, periodically jacking it up from the other side to take the pressure off, removing a few timbers, then lowering it farther, then repeating the procedure again and again until the safe was safely horizontal on the skid.

Lucky had the patience of Job; his sons, the numbness of Isaac.

Getting the skid from one end of the hall to the other was the easy part. As his sons pushed, Lucky placed more rollers of plastic pipe down in front of it. Once they reached the bottom of the steps, however, the pace slowed to glacial. The plan was to wrap a chain around the safe and another around the brick pier at the top of the stairs, connect them by means of a special winch — a "come-along" — then lever the safe up, step by step, securing each new position by inserting wooden wedges and tightening the come-along, notch by agonizing notch, until the safe had climbed the stairs. All, hopefully, without tearing down the house.

Every inch required half an hour of wedging, pulling, tying off, securing, wedging again. At various times, it looked as if the stairs, the rope, the chain, the crew, the brick pier, or all of them simultaneously would give way. The process took the entire day.

Thus were the pyramids built.

Then suddenly, at the moment of our triumph, and in the midst of the chaos, with *two days* left before the ball, Steve and I had to *leave*. Phil Donahue had invited us on his show to talk about the Pollock biography. We had to go to New York for a day. That meant leaving the project with no one in charge. If we closed it down, we would never finish in time. We chose to let it go on without us. Everyone knew what they had to do. What, we asked ourselves, could possibly go wrong in such a short time?

What, indeed.

The next day, during lunch, Mordia, king of the laborers, shared with Lee Lawrence, prince of the painters, the legend of the Whitney Silver. Big Macs and Quarter Pounders were abandoned in midbite as a half-dozen Lawrences scrambled to the basement to lay siege to the big vault. With trowels and scrapers, they tested the old walls until they found a loose brick, then another, then another. Finally, they broke through into cold darkness — a hole just big enough for a hand and a flashlight. When they saw nothing, they started widening the hole, brick by brick, until Lee pushed his way to the front and climbed in.

Everywhere he shined his flashlight, the beam fell on something shiny. But it wasn't silver. It was wine. Rows and rows of bottles, some still in wooden cases, filled the room. Later, when Steve and I picked through the rubble of what followed, we found fragments of labels: *Moët, Chandon, Mouton, Cadet, Rothschild, Margaux;* and dates: 1919, 1926, 1932, 1936 — a veritable archive of rare vintages from the best fields of the best wineries of the best regions in their best years.

To the Painting Lawrences, of course, it was "just a lot of old booze." They knew only that they had dug for four hours in the cold basement of Joye Cottage in search of silver and come up with not even an old coin to show for their trouble. Just a bunch of dusty bottles filled with dark old booze.

In a fury, they lobbed bottles through the opening they had made, out onto the concrete basement floor, where they shattered into emerald fragments. The crates they hauled upstairs and stacked in the huge ballroom fireplace. Somebody broke off the neck of a bottle, poured some of the maroon contents into a Hardee's *Wayne's World* plastic cup, and launched the rest across the room. Somebody else recognized one champagne label (*Dom Perignon*, 1936), and everyone wanted some of that. Now, instead of being broken full, bottles were sampled first. Someone ran across a rancid batch and spit it out in a great red shower of disgust. Everyone else did likewise.

The stack of old wooden cases in the fireplace somehow caught fire (afterward, no one admitted lighting the match), and a half-hearted attempt was made to rescue some bottles. But when the first one cracked and the wine sputtered out, smoking and hissing like acid, the rest were left to a similarly entertaining fate.

The combination of fire and booze, warmth and warmth, proved irresistible on a cold January evening, already dark, and the painters stayed long after quitting time, guzzling the musty old wine and piling more tinder on the sizzling blaze. The fire burned so hot that the bricks around the fireplace, after a century of the Whitneys' demure encampments, cracked and shivered as if new-laid. With their radios for once tuned to the same station, the Lawrences sang and shouted insults in the orange light. Full of wine and bravado, Lee clambered up a ladder to the ballroom rafters where he had been working and walked their thin edge from one side to the other as his cousins shouted encouragement from below.

When the night watchman — our temporary, low-tech "security system" and a superstitious man — came by to close up and saw the dancing silhouettes against the firelight, he turned and ran, thinking surely he had stumbled on some sort of satanic revelry.

The next day, Steve and I returned from New York, surveyed the damage, fired the painters, cleaned up the mess they left, and made our final preparations for the arrival of the Hunt's decorating crew the next morning. Much was still undone: no lights or appliances in the kitchen, no water in some wings, no heat anywhere. But the ballroom was plastered and painted, at least, and its great brass lanterns polished to a wondrous gleam. It would be a spartan affair — not exactly in the spirit of W.C. — but *grandly* spartan.

Late that night, the night before the ball, I ran into the watchman on his rounds. He wore a hat that looked vaguely like a train engineer's and a heavy, faded pea-green sweater that seemed slim protection from the unusual cold that had arrived, inevitably, just in time for our heatless party.

He said his usual "Ev'nin'" as we passed in the courtyard.

But my thoughts were elsewhere. The way the house looked in the moonlight reminded me of the night we arrived in Aiken, the night we first saw Joye Cottage: the facade filling the horizon from darkness to darkness, the ends so far distant from the center that they disappeared altogether, floating in moon shadow like some grand architectural ghost come back from the other side of demolition.

I sensed the watchman watching me. "Meta says you loves this house," he said.

I confessed. It was true.

"She says you believes in ghosts, too."

"In a sense," I said, surprising myself.

"Ole Mr. Whitney's still here, you know," the watchman said, as if confiding a great secret. "He died in this house."

Actually, according to all the official accounts, W. C. Whitney died from an attack of peritonitis during a performance of *Parsifal* at the Metropolitan Opera on January 28, 1904. Strangely, though, no one actually *saw* him at the opera that night, and his death wasn't announced until four days later. When reporters clamored for more details, none of the six doctors who treated him would make a public statement — the Whitney family had sworn them to secrecy.

"Don't you b'lieve what you reads in them books," the watchman admonished, reading my thoughts. "My father trained horses for Mr. Jock Whitney, and he told my father the *true* story." I knew Jock Whitney was W. C. Whitney's grandson — on the other side of the family, the side that had rejected W.C. in favor of Oliver Payne's millions. "Mr. Jock said his grandfather was shot to death in this house right here."

Shot to death? I suddenly remembered that even the official accounts of Whitney's life referred to "deep suspicions" about the strange official version of his death, and that other versions circulated madly at the time — including one that Whitney had been shot.

According to the watchman's version, W.C. never went to the opera that night. He wasn't even in New York on January 28, 1904. He was in Aiken, at Joye Cottage — "in that room right there," said the watchman, pointing to the window of the room we knew had once been Whitney's. Apparently, W.C. was "getting biblical" with a female houseguest when her husband walked in and found them in flagrante. Whereupon the husband pulled out a pistol and shot his host "in the offendin' region."

Whitney was placed on his private train and rushed back to New York, according to the watchman's story, but "bled to his death" on the way.

"And I suppose his ghost returned to Joye Cottage," I supplied.

"Who said anything about ghosts?" said the watchman, shaking his head scornfully.

46.

Home at Last

Renovate it, and they will come.

And come they did. Not in carriages, but in cars. Not in Shelby-seated Lincoln limousines, but in Mercedeses and Explorers and panel-sided station wagons — the preferred cars of the inheriting class. They came and parked like any other party goers and crunched their way across our gravel driveway, the women holding their long skirts, the men holding their women. But once they began to stream through the massive front door and into the amber light, it was suddenly 1897 again: sequined gowns and piqué vests;

diamond tiaras and golden cuff links; taffeta and brocade and mink and cashmere; silk scarves and satin lapels.

Standing in the entrance hall watching this stately, sumptuous procession, I felt, for just a moment, like old Mr. Whitney. He, too, had rushed his team of workmen through a gauntlet of construction, defying the calendar and common sense, turning a caprice into a cliff-hanger, all for a *party*. All to make Joye Cottage ready for his Christmas bash — I remembered the ashen wreath, "Merry Christmas, W.C."— and, of course, for Edith.

To look at the guests, some of whose grandparents had shared the same halls with the "new" Mrs. Whitney, it really could have been 1897. Except there were no liveried servants welcoming them at the door. Marge, the prison warden, and Desmond "Tina Turner" Harris (rehired just for the occasion) took coats. There were no private train cars crowded on the siding at the railroad station, only a leased plane or two at the Aiken airport, and just a sprinkling of the grand names — Hitchcock and Burden and Goodyear and, of course, Whitney — of a New York society that survived mostly in the form of endowments and trust funds.

And instead of W. C. Whitney's tall, commanding figure at the head of the receiving line, there was only Steve and me, looking dapper (we were told) in black-tie and white-tie, respectively; but underneath our smiles and satin lapels, exhausted, anxious, and ready to collapse.

Which was roughly the condition of Joye Cottage, too.

Despite all our manic, Marx Brothers efforts to get the house ready in time, much of the major work had to be left undone — that is, if you call heat, water, electricity, plumbing, and plaster "major." Only the ballroom, in fact, was really ready, and even it had dribbles and swirls and spills of paint on the floor where the Lawrence cousins, drunk on 1927 *Château Merlot,* had furiously debated Jackson Pollock's genius.

Yet when the guests began to arrive and make their stately, milling procession through the half-finished rooms — rooms that only the day before had been filled with carpenters and plasterers and electricians — *they noticed nothing.* Nothing except a grand setting for a memorable party, a setting so elegant and festive that even W.C., the ultimate party giver, would have approved.

What kind of magic was this? How did we pull such a resplendent rabbit out of what had been, only the day before, such a horrific hat?

We didn't. Joan Tower did.

The former mistress of Joye Cottage and field marshal of the Hunt's decorating committee had ridden to our rescue with what she called "bedouin baroque." She and her crew of Hunt decoratrixes (along with some of our workers whom she dragooned into service) had draped every unpainted and, in some cases, unplastered wall with hundreds of yards of fabric — muslin and chintz, plain and striped — creating one exotically tented room after another. Silk moiré covered stained plaster; jade velvet hid virgin plywood; and gold lamé, sprinkled with rose petals, cascaded down the battered salon stairs (so convincingly that the *Town & Country* photographer chose it as her backdrop). To cover the seams, Joan hung riding prints and garlands of ribbons, and everywhere, extravaganzas of flowers. The effect was somewhere between *The Arabian Nights,* a garden party at Buckingham Palace, a tent wedding, and a state fair.

But it worked.

No amount of silk moiré or gold lamé or ribbons or floral bouquets, however, could hide the temperature. Earlier that evening, around six-thirty, Steve and I had anxiously dialed the weather. It was twenty-five degrees. After that, we called every five minutes, praying for a sudden heat wave. We got just the opposite. The temperature fell a degree every half hour. By nine, when guests started arriving, removing their furs to reveal alarming expanses of bare back and shoulder, not to mention plunging necklines, the thermometer was plunging into the teens. And that didn't count the wind, which kicked up after sunset, of course, chilling the bones to something more like ten. Someone assured us that this was extraordinary weather for South Carolina — indeed, it would probably set a record.

We found that cold comfort.

In anticipation of just such arctic conditions — and out of guilt for not having the furnace up and running in time — the heating contractor had supplied us with three Salamander stoves, long, torpedolike heaters that blew a fierce blast of hot air the length of a football field. "These babies can warm up even the coldest construction site," he assured us. We had to take this on faith, however, because they arrived too late (Murphy at work, one last time) for us to try them out before the party. Tonight was their maiden flight.

It was a crash and burn. They might have been able to warm up even the coldest construction site, but we were a *ball,* not a barn raising. It wasn't that they didn't give off enough heat. Just the opposite. They gave off gigawatts of heat. Hiroshimas of heat. Solar flares of heat. And their fierce jet exhaust wreaked havoc with expensive hairdos and layered petticoats alike, turning every hapless dowager who crossed their path into an unwilling Marilyn Monroe on the subway grate in *The Seven-Year Itch.* And the noise! A fearsome, screaming whine, like an F-18 streaking past at treetop level directly overhead, accompanied by a rumble and bellow as if the earth would crack. What the blasts of hot air did to clothes and coifs, the noise did to conversation. When all three engines were running, the sound was like Armageddon — or at least the long-feared Soviet attack.

Between their insufferable heat, cataclysmic wind, and apocalyptic sound, the Salamanders cut a swath of chaos no matter which way we pointed them. So we did the only thing we could do, cold or no cold. We turned them off.

That left only one source of heat. Only one way for 250 guests to warm themselves — the same way that guests in Joye Cottage had been warming themselves since the days of Sarah Joye and her little country inn; since before that, when the kitchen wing was a farmhouse overlooking the field where "Fighting Joe" Wheeler won his rare Confederate victory against Sherman's advancing bluecoats; and even before that, when the ground under us was nothing but a grassy, treeless plain stretching all the way to the Atlantic, and Creek and Cherokee Indians huddled against the cold winds that must have blown then. Our guests, like all their predecessors on this spot of ground, stood by the fire.

First in small groups, then in larger and larger huddles, they gathered around one of the five fires that burned through the night, as fast and furiously as we could stoke them.

But there was no fire in the kitchen. And no heat. And no electricity, except for one bare lightbulb that cast a merciless glare on a scene of utter panic as the caterer and her staff raced through the cold and dark trying desperately to prepare an elegant, *hot*, sit-down dinner for 250. "Whoever invented Hell," sputtered Ginny Huckabee, the brave caterer who had accepted this assignment, "wasn't a cook. If a cook had invented Hell, it wouldn't be a hot place, it would be a bitter-cold place," she said, looking around at the steam rising from her pans of lobster Newburg like fog off a Maine pond on a winter morning. *"Like this!"*

And, no doubt, would have been similarly equipped. The room Ginny was panicking in was a kitchen in name only. Except for paint thinner and brass polish, the cupboards were stone bare: not so much as a teaspoon of sugar or a pinch of salt in sight. If she didn't bring it with her, she did without. In fact, there was only one thing that we *did* have. And we had it in abundance.

Refrigeration.

Not surprisingly, the call to dinner came early, and the fireside congregations reluctantly melted away as guests sought out their table assignments. It wasn't until then that some of them learned the shocking news: They would be eating *outside*. To accommodate the larger-than-expected turnout, Madame Tower and her crew had draped *the porch* — the grand, hundred-foot-long veranda with its sweeping colonnade overlooking the courtyard — in striped canvas. True, on a balmy spring night, the veranda would have made a lovely spot for a candlelit dinner: the moon on the reflecting pool, the ballroom windows aglow, the pines murmuring, a sweet hint of tea olive on the breeze. And, in fact, Joan had draped the canvas in such a way that it could be rolled up if the weather permitted.

It didn't.

Like ships' captains determined to go down with their vessel, Steve and I took our seats on the porch, surrounded by canvas walls that flapped madly with every gust of arctic air, bald-headed men and bare-shouldered women struggling to maintain their aristocratic composure under conditions never imagined by Emily Post, and a Salamander heater, finally turned back on in desperation, that rumbled and bellowed to no discernible effect. By the time the baked Alaska arrived, Steve and I were the only ones left at our table. Inside my patent leather shoes and thin socks, I had lost the feeling in my toes.

But none of that mattered once the dancing began.

It wasn't 1897, of course. We didn't have a Hungarian orchestra (only a four-piece band from Augusta), and the magical swish from all those whirling petticoats was missing. But if you squinted your eyes, the amber glow from the big brass carriage lamps could have been candlelight, and the wailing blues could have been a waltz. And the sound of feet on the pine floor was the same. And the firelight.

And the laughter.

But so much had happened inside these walls in the century since W.C. and Edith first danced here.

Not being dancers ourselves, Steve and I spent most of the evening talking about the *Donahue* appearance or explaining *why* a biography of Jackson Pollock. But every once in a while, I would catch myself looking into the fire and imagining the scene I had missed just a few nights before: the Lawrence cousins and their work-site *Walpurgisnacht*. They, at least, had solved the mystery of the vault, if not that of the silver. And they, too, had danced.

And I remembered the mischievous teenagers who used to break into the house when it was empty and neck in the windows and play their radios in this same room. They danced, too.

And Eugene, on his scaffold, jumping up and down, stalking back and forth in a gavotte of rage. And Mordia, whose mind danced. And Meta, whose eyes danced.

We'd been giving a ball all this time and didn't even know it.

Quietly, when no one was looking, we slipped out onto the ballroom porch, where the frigid air was suddenly bracing and welcome after so much fire and closeness. We could see the whole house from the edge of the porch: the window of Edith's bedchamber, where the cabbage roses were; W.C.'s fatal trysting room; the salon where Caruso sang, Fred Astaire danced, and our mysterious houseguest slept in the window seat.

Then we looked back through the ballroom window at the amber-lit dancers.

And we felt home.

At Home

That was a year ago.

The house is finished now. Mostly. There is one wing with five guest rooms that we haven't tackled yet. The ten bedrooms we have seem sufficient for now, although when both our families come, the house tends to fill up quickly, just as it did for William Whitney. We joke that if nieces and nephews multiply too rapidly, we may need to do what W.C. did: add on. We have, in fact, already added one room by enclosing a screen porch to give us a sitting area off the kitchen. This prompted guffaws of disbelief among our friends: "What? You need *more* space?"

The painters and plasterers are gone now. The wood-working shop that filled our salon with stacks of lumber, sawdust, and inconceivable noise is gone. A huge Oriental carpet covers the floor where so many muddy boots used to tramp on their way to the morning's tasks; a grand piano sits where the table saw used to; and a grouping of tufted chairs covered in sky-blue damask where the planer made its horrendous racket.

The workers have left, but their work remains. That's the best thing about work, a plumber's or a writer's: It survives long after the worker is gone. Bad work, of course, can spoil the best memories, but good work can renovate the worst. Take Eugene, for example. He is long gone, and his antics with him. But his art still surrounds us — in the beautiful plaster medallions, the dentil moldings and egg-and-dart cornices, to say nothing of the ubiquitous mirror-smooth walls. The carpenters, Bart and Manny and the rest, are gone now, too, probably off in the woods hunting some un-suspecting deer with an assault rifle and a night scope. But the staircases and the paneling and the mahogany book-cases they built are all still here, bearing square and level witness to the wonders that can be wrought with a good eye, a few tools, and a lot of noise.

Even the security system, after so many false starts, is a thing of beauty. Eventually, we found somebody who could make sense of the Gordian knot of loose wires and limp ex-cuses that had left us insecure for so long. Now, every door and window in the house is wired and every room moni-tored by a system that keeps constant watch. And God help the burglar who sets off the alarm: a huge, piercing scream of noise from a dozen sirens that would surely wake the ghost of Edith Whitney.

No, we haven't seen the ghost yet. Although we can't seem to get rid of that leak in the Weeping Room and can't seem to find the cause, either. We know what Meta would say about that.

Work inside may have stopped, but the project goes on. A task equal to refurbishing the house was refurnishing it, and that task, too, remains unfinished. Needless to say, the holdovers from our Bauhaus New York apartment were spread pretty thin in ten times more space and fifteen times as many rooms. Fortunately, thanks to its prewar wealth (that's the Civil War, for those who haven't been paying attention), the South is a great place to buy antiques, especially Federal and Empire styles; and we have discovered several regional auction houses that are the antiquarian equivalent of Frank Hatch's hairstyling emporium: New York quality at very un–New York prices.

Speaking of things un–New York, we finally found someone to take care of Joye Cottage. Mrs. Johnson took her Anti-Dust campaign back to Tennessee, Marge returned to prison (as an employee, that is), and Desmond went back to his leather miniskirts. In their exalted place, we have Pete and Olivia, a young couple who, between them, keep the inside of the house immaculate and the outside groomed. We hope someday soon to have them move into the second floor of the kitchen wing where we've left eight small staff bedrooms in the bombed-out state to which our demolitionist, Lionel, reduced them. Someday, it will make a comfortable apartment — even a palatial one by New York standards.

Pete not only mows the grass and clips the hedges and cleans out the gutters, he does all the shopping. That includes not just the makings for Olivia's meals but enough cleaning supplies, toilet paper, and — Mrs. Miller forgive us — paper towels for three kitchens and thirteen bathrooms. During the winter, it's Pete's job to keep fires built in all eighteen fireplaces. Of all the many joys of Joye Cottage, none is sweeter than lighting a hardwood fire on a cold (forty-degree) night. In an instant, in the flare of a match, we can recapture another century, and in the amber light, W.C. and Edith roam the house again.

Pete also cleans the windows — the outsides, anyway; Olivia cleans the insides. There are 138 windows in the house, which, thanks to the diamond-paned upper sashes, adds up to more than four thousand individual panes. In New York, keeping all of them clean would have been a full-time job. Even in our bunker on Central Park West, which didn't face any street, two weeks was as long as a good cleaning lasted. (If the air did that to the windows, what was it doing to our lungs?) But the air, like everything else, is different in Aiken. Pete and Olivia wash the windows twice a year here. And they're never dirty.

Olivia also does the laundry and cleans the house. The former job is made easier by our preference in clothes: shorts and T-shirts in summer; sweats in winter. Period. We've even stopped dressing up for company. Just too much trouble. The only way to make the laundry easier would be to turn Joye Cottage into a nudist camp. Hmmm. Olivia's other job, keeping the house clean, is also aided tremendously by our insistence that guests take their shoes off at the door. After an initial hue and cry of protest — especially from older friends and women in dresses — everyone now accepts our "socks only" policy.

And the rule applies to everyone. No exceptions.

Late one night, before the security system was completed, I heard someone in the house and opened my bedroom door to see a policeman standing in the hall, flashlight in hand. "I was driving by and saw one of your doors open," he said.

"You'll have to take your shoes off," I said, looking down disapprovingly at his service boots. Burglars could wait; the boots couldn't.

It hasn't always been that easy, of course. Not long ago, we hosted a meeting of the Junior Student Club, a local ladies' club that has met every month, without interruption, since 1934. The group's membership is limited to twenty-four, so a member has to move or die for a new member to be admitted. As a result, the median age is somewhere in the seventies. And the oldest member is over a hundred. Would we make a hundred-year-old woman take off her shoes? This was truly a test of our resolve.

Fortunately, it never came to a confrontation. Having been warned in advance about our Japanese shoe policy, the women came with bedroom slippers in hand. Even the centenarian refused special treatment and insisted on wearing a pair of fuzzy pink bunnies she had bought specially for the occasion.

Large groups of guests, of course, produce equally large piles of shoes. Some people, like the ladies of the Student Club, don't mind the Filene's Basement crush at the door when the party's over. Indeed, some guests take advantage of the opportunity to try a new look ("Ooh, these are just my size!"). Once a guest called up after returning home to report that she had *somebody else's* black pumps on. One frequent visitor has suggested that we avoid this problem by installing a shoe rack big enough for every guest to have his or her own slot, complete with personalized name tag — like the place card at a dinner party. Regular guests, of course, would have permanent slots, with brass name-plates, where they could keep their own personal slippers at the ready. To dress it up still further — and encourage compliance — the same friend suggested that we install a few fake plates — Q. Elizabeth II, B. Streisand, E. Presley.

With work inside the house at a halt, our restless attention has turned to the five acres of land around us, which suffered at least as much neglect at the hands of Mr. Kane as the house. Nature, of course, has a way of maintaining itself, of imposing its own order, even if it isn't the one we had in mind. When we arrived, fiercely barbed smilax vines were overwhelming the manicured cherry hedges. Fragrant, lovely, and treacherous wisteria were strangling the trees. The once-beautiful box garden off the ballroom had lost most of its box and hardly looked like a garden at all. But slowly — more slowly than the house; you can't nail limbs back on a tree — we are reclaiming these, too, for a while, from the implacable armies of Time.

Speaking of time, we're back to working the same long, perversely inverted hours that we did in New York (up at dusk, to bed at dawn — I tell friends I'm on Hawaiian time). During the months of renovation, both Steve and I defied the writer's most fundamental instinct — to sleep

in — and greeted the first workers at the door every day when the sun was barely up. It wasn't that hard. The excitement and anticipation of the work ahead was enough to catapult us out of bed every morning at hours that used to mark the end of the day, not the beginning. (The thought of forty-dollar-an-hour electricians standing around with nothing to do helped.) What *was* hard, for the same reason, was getting to sleep at night, what with visions of paneling and cornices and marble mantels dancing in our heads.

So now we're back to our old schedule, although, frankly, keeping Hawaiian time isn't as easy as it used to be. In Manhattan, we never felt that we were the only ones awake, no matter how late the hour. In Aiken, midnight feels lonely. On long summer days, the pool beckons; in winter, the warm southern sun. And in every season, day or night, the lure of quiet country lanes lined with dogwoods and canopied in fragrant magnolias is an irresistible alternative to the flickering gray light of a computer monitor.

One thing's for sure: In New York, we never had to give tours.

Now, it seems, we spend most of our free time showing people around the house. Hardly a week goes by that friends don't call to say they have guests in town who would *love* to see Joye Cottage. I'm always reminded of how out-of-town visitors to New York were forever dragging me to see the Statue of Liberty or the Empire State Building — sights that I never would have seen on my own. Well, now *we* are the Statue of Liberty — by Aiken standards, anyway.

If we *had* given tours of our bunker on Central Park West, they would have lasted no more than three minutes. You could see every room in the apartment without leaving the front hall. But Joye Cottage is a different story. A fully annotated tour (we call it the five-dollar package) can take an hour and a half, drinks not included. Still, there is a certain pleasure in asking an American businessman with a billion dollars or an English nobleman with a great country house (both of whom have, indeed, visited) to please take off his shoes.

In short, we've gotten used to living here. Despite all the doomsaying of New York acquaintances and our own fretting, we have a more active social life here than we ever had in the Big Apple. There, we had to schedule even a casual evening with friends three weeks in advance. Here, we are far more likely to get a late call suggesting a quick trip for pizza. And getting there is a whole lot easier. Indeed, everything is easier here: from shopping for food

(twenty-four hours) to seeing a movie (no lines); from fixing a car (no hassles) to buying socks (something we do
often).

And yes, despite our early travails with barbecue, we
have even found a few good restaurants — very good ones,
in fact. The food they feature can't exactly be described as
indigenous (one chef is from San Diego; another trained in
Tuscany), but good food is good food. Picturesque is for
postcards.

We've even gotten used to living in sixty rooms. Hard to
believe, I know. So used to it, in fact, that sometimes we
wonder how we ever got along in less. (In New York, we
used to dream about how a *fifth* room would change our
lives.) Between the offices in the ballroom wing for the re-
searchers who help us with our books, our own offices on
the second floor, the kitchen at one end of the house, and
our bedrooms at the other (a football field away), we see
just about every room except the guest rooms at least once a
day. Getting used to, even blasé, about sixty rooms was so
easy that we wonder sometimes if any house is so big that
you wouldn't get used to it sooner or later. I'll bet the queen
of England walks around Buckingham Palace, with its 479
rooms (*eight* Joye Cottages) and thinks, "Hey, this ain't so
big."

We do miss the renovation, though.

I never thought I would say this, but there's a part of us
that misses it. Sure, there was mess and noise and stress and
expense (kind of like New York, come to think of it). But
there was also discovery and accomplishment and community (like the best of families). We miss it so much, in fact,

that we're aching to start work again. Cousin Robert has already drawn up plans for the next and final phase of renovations. And when that's done, we hope to add a screening room and gym in the basement.

And when that's done, there's this 120-room house in Massachusetts . . .

Acknowledgments

Hard though it is to believe, we did not spin this book out of thin air. Among the many friends and neighbors who shared with us their knowledge of Aiken, its history, and its people, we should thank Kiki Blalock, Sandy Cassatt, Liz Kasner, Don Law, Rosamond McDuffie, Lucky Dale Meissinger, Annie Mitchell, Buddy Raines, Jack and Liz Seabrook, Joan Tower, and others who probably prefer to remain anonymous anyway.

Even harder to believe is that we read some books in preparing our story. In particular, we should acknowledge Kay Lawrence's *Heroes, Horses & High Society: Aiken from*

1540 (King Press, 1971); and Will Cole's *The Many Faces of Aiken: A Pictorial History* (The Donning Company, 1985); as well as two fine biographies of the builder of Joye Cottage: W. A. Swanberg's *Whitney Father, Whitney Heiress* (Charles Scribner's Sons, 1980); and Mark D. Hirsch's *William C. Whitney: Modern Warwick* (Archon Books, 1969). Of all the many books on the Gilded Age we read, by far the most helpful was Mary Cable's elegantly written and extraordinarily insightful *Top Drawer: American High Society from the Gilded Age to the Roaring Twenties* (Atheneum, 1984). If only all history were so graceful and intelligent.

Finally, we should thank (and exculpate) the brave friends and family who read the manuscript at various stages of completion, and offered advice that we occasionally had the wisdom to heed: Tim Arwood; Gordon Atkinson; Kiki Blalock; Marsh and Lisa Burckhalter; Latham and Paddy Ann Burns; John Cahill; Linda Chevalier; Brent Cline; Darrell Engle; Sarah Fitzsimmons; Chris Greame; Joe Hartzler; Jon Jackson; Loretta Jerdan; Kathryn Madden; Rosamond McDuffie; George, Marion, and Carolyn Naifeh; Pete Negrete; Dan Ranger; Robert Rich; Liz Seabrook; William and Kathryn Smith; Lucy Stec; Deanna Tremlin; Beverly Veasey; Melissa Westerdahl; Susan Yarborough; Bill Yount; and Leigh Anne Zalants. Steve's father, George Naifeh, not only read the book, but spent many hours combing the Whitney papers at the Library of Congress for mentions of Joye Cottage.

We are also enormously grateful to all the people at Little, Brown who worked with us on this book, first among them Fredi Friedman, our editor, who read the manuscript repeatedly, always challenging us to improve it, and making many critical recommendations along the way. She is also responsible for leading us to the final title for the book, and for that we are grateful, too.

Also at Little, Brown, we would like to thank the publisher, Charles Hayward, as well as Peggy Freudenthal, Caroline Hagen, Jacquie Miller, Lisa Singer, and Steve Snider, all of whom worked so hard to make this book both an artistic and a commercial success. Our heartfelt gratitude, also, to Daniel Baxter, the illustrator, who helped bring so many of the images in the book to life.